M000247585

THE COMMUNITY BANK SURVIVAL GUIDE

THE COMMUNITY BANK SURVIVAL GUIDE

Overcoming the Challenges of an Increasingly Competitive Marketplace

DR. DOUGLAS V. AUSTIN

President and CEO
Austin Financial Services, Inc.

Boston, Massachusetts   Burr Ridge, Illinois
Dubuque, Iowa   Madison, Wisconsin   New York, New York
San Francisco, California   St. Louis, Missouri

Library of Congress Cataloging-in-Publication Data

Austin, Douglas V.
  The Community Bank Survival Guide: Overcoming the Challenges of an Increasingly
  Competitive Marketplace / Douglas V. Austin.
      p.   cm.
  Includes index.
  ISBN   0-7863-1107-X
  1. Community banks—United States.   2. Banks and banking—United
States.   I. Title.
HG2491.A97   1997
332.3'0973—dc20   96–31160

McGraw·Hill

A Division of The McGraw·Hill Companies

© 1998 by The McGraw-Hill Companies, Inc. All rights reserved. Printed in the
United States of America. Except as permitted under the United States Copyright
Act of 1976, no part of this publication may be reproduced or distributed in any
form or by any means, or stored in a data base or retrieval system, without the prior
written permission of the publisher.

3 4 5 6 7 8 9 BKM BKM   9 0 9 8 7 6 5 4 3 2 1 0

McGraw-Hill books are available at special quantity discounts to use as premiums
and sales promotions, or for use in corporate training programs. For more
information, please write to the Director of Special Sales, McGraw-Hill, 11 West
19th Street, New York, NY 10011. Or contact your local bookstore.

Information contained in this work has been obtained by The McGraw-Hill Companies, Inc.
("McGraw-Hill") from sources believed to be reliable. However, neither McGraw-Hill nor
its authors guarantees the accuracy or completeness of any information published herein and
neither McGraw-Hill nor its authors shall be responsible for any errors, omissions, or
damages arising out of use of this information. This work is published with the
understanding that McGraw-Hill and its authors are supplying information but are not
attempting to render engineering or other professional services. If such services are required,
the assistance of an appropriate professional should be sought.

This book is dedicated to my wife, Gayle Joyce Austin. For better or worse, and for all the times in between, she has been my partner for over 32 years.

CONTENTS

Chapter 14

Management Competency and Compensation   110

Chapter 15

Board and Management Education   123

Chapter 16

The Future of Community Banks and Thrifts in the International, National, and Interstate Banking and Branching Environment   134

PREFACE

This book starts out with a discussion of abolishing tradition in community banking. Tradition must be replaced by change. Tradition can be the death knell of community banking. Chapter 2 discusses what a community bank is, how it can survive, and how it must survive as a financial intermediary. The following chapter, Chapter 3, outlines visioning—which is strategic planning squared. Visioning is the overall, forward-looking analysis for your community bank/thrift and its place within the community in the far years to come, not just two or three years ahead. If you do not have a vision, you cannot come up with a strategic plan for tomorrow.

Commencing with Chapter 4, we analyze the various techniques for surviving as a community bank/thrift. The financial and corporate flexibility outlined by bank and thrift holding companies is discussed in detail in Chapter 4. For those community banks/thrifts that are in stock form, Chapter 5 emphasizes shareholder relations, shareholder corporate redemption policies, and overall shareholder communications as ways of keeping your shareholders loyal and your financial institution out of the hands of unwanted suitors.

Chapter 6 outlines the importance of financial and managerial leadership for your community bank/thrift and how you must develop techniques to provide such leadership for your community. In Chapter 7, techniques for improving internal and external growth of your financial intermediary are noted to help you survive as a financial institution. In this same vein, Chapter 8 outlines the importance of the new sales and marketing culture to the community bank/thrift as the most important technique for its survival as a financial intermediary. The industry is no longer a series of order takers, but must be a proactive, assertive, and aggressive marketing financial institution that meets the challenges of other financial service corporations head on, day in and day out, in every aspect of the market.

Chapter 9 discusses the importance of profitability, capital adequacy, and asset and liability management as a means of survivability. This chapter, along with others within the manuscript, highlights how to survive—not whether you will survive as a financial intermediary.

Chapter 10 outlines how to meet the regulatory burdens faced by community banks and thrifts on a day-to-day basis at the state and federal levels, how to work within the system, and how not only to survive, but to thrive amid such regulatory scrutiny.

Chapters 11 and 12 highlight the utilization of technology as a modern technique for providing profitability and the services to survive. In Chapter 12, the scope of products and services to be provided, and the emphasis on profitability of such products and services are addressed. Tradition must be scrapped so that the new products and services provided—whether by human beings or through the technologies stressed in Chapter 11—are profitable and provide a meaningful service to the public to be accommodated.

The final portion of the book highlights the role of the board of directors and what it must do to provide the necessary emphasis and impetus for survival. The role of the board of directors—not as a group facing liabilities and responsibilities, but as a group of individuals responsible for the supervision and direction of the institution in a safe and solvent manner—is outlined; the duties to provide such administration are highlighted. The point of Chapter 13 is not to discuss liabilities and responsibilities but to highlight what techniques are necessary from the board's perspective to assist the management and staff in providing safe and solvent banking. Chapters 14 and 15 discuss the importance of more than adequate management competency and compensation and the means by which the board and management are educated in order to provide the appropriate leadership and administration. If the management is not competent, the community bank/thrift will not survive; the easiest way by which to provide adequate and competent management is to provide them with more than adequate compensation. As important as compensation is education, year to year, as the industry changes and becomes more complex. Chapter 15 emphasizes the importance of management and board education as well as the sources available to directors and managers for such education throughout the United States.

Finally, Chapter 16 highlights what I believe the year 2000 will look like to banking and how the community bank/thrift can survive until then and beyond if it attempts to meet the requirements of the previous chapters of this manuscript. Not all financial institutions will survive—however, there is no reason why your institution cannot survive if you decide to follow the recommendations made in this book.

THE COMMUNITY BANK SURVIVAL GUIDE

CHAPTER 1

Eliminating Tradition
Change, Change, Change

While "tradition" may be one of the finest songs from the Broadway musical *Fiddler on the Roof*, it is a killer at community financial institutions. Tradition breeds comfort, sloth, inattention, and lack of intelligence. As a bank consultant for the past 30 years, this author finds tradition and its synonyms ("we've always done it this way," "it's our standard procedure," and "it has always worked in the past") to be the number one cause for not keeping up with the industry standards and not being a progressive financial intermediary. Tradition breeds relaxation and apathy. It takes away the uncertainty, risk, and competitiveness of the marketplace. Tradition prevents the board of directors and senior management from realizing the exact nature and competitive forces facing them in their own industry and from outside. Tradition has the tendency to veil economic and financial threats in the eyes of the board and management; often the board/ management has to react to economic and financial conditions within its marketplace, or even worse, within the financial institution itself, that could have been easily cleaned up and remedied earlier when the community financial institution had been in a proactive rather than a reactive stance.

Why is tradition so deadly to the survival of a community financial institution? It is because it makes responsible people irresponsible. It is very similar to the old adage, "If it ain't broke, don't fix it." Many community banking organizations operate profitably, have more than adequate capital, and have competent personnel who operate the bank or thrift on a day-to-day basis with very few problems. State and federal regulatory agencies praise the financial institution for its conformity with every state and federal law possible, and there are no major impediments to survival. Several years of this type of ambiance within the community bank or thrift will lead to apathy and possibly death. It makes everybody feel comfortable and positive as to the fact they are doing everything right—year after year this builds up a tradition that hinders change and even the possibility of examining new ways to do things. Furthermore, if there is not much employee/management/director turnover, new ideas are not fostered, and the minds of the individuals become similar to the old LaBrea Tar Pits rather than a bubbling stew.

Over the past 30 years, I have seen banks and thrifts whose major problem was that they were not thinking ahead. In the next several chapters, we will talk about the survivability of the independent community-banking–oriented institutions as well as the importance of strategic planning, but in this chapter, let me just start out by discussing the problem of not thinking at all. Your management runs a bank profitably and safely day-to-day; the board of directors supervises and monitors the bank or thrift day-to-day with insignificant problems arising—and they are quickly remedied; and no one pays attention to the fork in the road coming up, the stop light ahead, or even worse, a brick wall facing the financial institution. As Tom Peters has said, it's like planning and looking through the rear view mirror of your car, rather than through the windshield. You don't try to plan into the future, but simply act day-to-day based upon the activities of the past. More than once while consulting with community banks and thrifts, I have been told flat out that we don't need to do such and such because we have never done it before and everything is OK. This is extremely prevalent where management has never worked anywhere else than in the financial institution in question. The most important aspect of management education through schooling at state, regional, and national trade associations, proprietary seminars, and so on is for the bankers and thrift managers to meet and interact with others within the industry who do not necessarily perform the same tasks the same way. Over half of the education at a conference comes from talking with others who are peers rather than simply listening to the lectures. A bank with a tradition is one that says, "Why should we split the stock, since we have never split the stock?"—needless to say, a $4,000 book value may not be a very reasonable price for attempting to sell 100 share blocks to new shareholders. Another tradition-oriented philosophy is the answer when asked why the financial institution is not in the secondary mortgage market—"Because we have never been in the past." The real answer would have been, "We have nobody who has the expertise to handle the paperwork to be in the secondary market," but that answer is never given—it's simply, "Well, we've never done it in the past and we are not going to do it now."

Tradition is all around you. It permeates the corporate life of your community bank. It has become the "rebar" of your brick and mortar. It must be torn down through the implementation of aggressive, proactive management and supervision in order for the community bank to survive. Let's look at a couple of characteristics of the tradition-bound community financial institution:

- A board of directors that averages in excess of 60 years of age.
- A board of directors whose average term of service is over 20 years.
- A senior management that has been in place 10 to 15 years or more.
- Senior management that has seen no new blood from outside in the past 10 years.
- A staff of the community bank that has only been given on-the-job training with no emphasis for staff and management education.
- No examination of possible branch sites or mergers over the past 10 years.
- No new products and services implemented by the bank in the past five years.
- No senior management members who have gone to regional or national banking schools.
- Main office hasn't been redecorated in the past decade.
- Secretaries are still using IBM Selectric typewriters.

I could go on and on, but I think I've made the point. In order for your "bank" to meet the challenges of the next 5, 10, or 15 years, you have to be looking forward to changes that are facing you today and even tomorrow. Furthermore, you have to (1) meet the challenges of today and tomorrow, (2) have a highly educated, proactive staff, and (3) maintain physical facilities and products and services that are on the cutting edge. You may never be able to provide the wide range of services of a Nations Bank or a Bank One, but you may not have to. On the other hand, you may have to provide secondary mortgage services, financial consulting, discount brokerage, and the sale of mutual funds and annuities in order to remain competitive within your marketplace. Each of your markets will be different and each of your financial institutions is different. However, failure to think ahead, plan aggressively, and keep an open mind concerning change will throttle your ability to succeed in the long run.

As you are quite aware, the only thing certain about the future is change. What we are doing today will not be what we are doing tomorrow, and the people who are doing it today won't be here tomorrow to do it. The board of directors will change, the management will retire or move on to other financial institutions, and your staff will retire. Furthermore, the senior lending officer's job five years from now will be different that it is today. The CFO will have different responsibilities five years from now than he or she has today. The delivery systems that you will utilize in the years to come will be different than the delivery systems you use today. The types of banking offices may be physically larger or smaller, the office may be open more or less hours, and the use of technology and electronics may be the bulk of your delivery system by the year 2000 rather than brick and mortar branches. Your market is unique, and you will have to adapt to the needs of your customers, rather than vice versa. However, change should not be undertaken simply for the sake of change. The fact that the bank down the street is doing something (i.e. selling mutual funds and annuities) does not mean that you should be selling mutual funds and annuities. Change should be researched. Change should be analyzed. Change should be a result of a business judgment of the board of directors and senior management. Change is proactive, not a knee-jerk reaction to what your competitors are doing or what you have read in the *American Banker*, *The Wall Street Journal*, or your local state trade organization newsletter. For example, one of the latest hot items is imaging. There are countless salespersons representing quality firms beating the bushes of banking America to sell imaging to your financial institution. The fact that the bank down the street has bought an imaging system doesn't mean that you have to. You don't have to be the first bank or thrift in your market to buy the imaging system. However, if you have done a cost–benefit analysis and imaging becomes cost-efficient, then installation of an imaging system assists you in delivering services to your customers more efficiently and less expensively than if you did not have imaging.

Let's take another example: Should your computers be internal or should you use an outside data processor? Community financial institutions are all over the block on this subject. Size does not seem indicative of whether you have operations processed internally or whether you use a data service bureau. Justification for housing a computer and its ancillary people within your organization is often based upon "keeping up with the Joneses" or the selling ability of some salesperson. Over the years, bank managements felt that they needed to have an internal computer in order to get the "right" types of reports. It was impossible to get the management information from a data service bureau. That has been determined to be nonsense. Specific management reports are capable of being downloaded onto PCs and these reports can then be massaged internally even if you use a data processor. Furthermore, many data processing service bureaus are capable of customizing management reports even though they serve 50 or hundreds of banks and thrifts in a vast geographic area. The question of whether the computer should be internal or external is really a question of cost and effectiveness of the results achieved. Consider this scenario: Your bank is running out of physical space in the main office and may have to build a 50 percent larger addition. At the same time, the computers utilized by the internal operations department are now economically obsolete. They are going to have to be replaced by either leasing or buying new computers. These are not two separate transactions—they are the flipside of the same transaction. If a cost–benefit study indicates that the utilization of an outside data service bureau would be more cost-efficient and provide quality operational service, then the elimination of the computer department internally might free up enough space to eliminate the need for a new addition to the main office. Alternatively, there is no need today with electronic banking, technology, fax machines, and telephones for the operational department (i.e., the computer area) to be in the main office. Instead of building a new addition to the main office, throw the computer department into one of your branches that has excess space. The old IBM motto is: "Think, Think, Think." Every problem has a potential solution that may not be the traditional solution that you have given it for the past two decades. Your survival may depend upon a new approach to thinking out the solution, a solution that is heretical to what you have done in the past and breaks the mold with finality.

As you read this book, do it with an open mind and subject your thinking to new ideas and concepts. If you broaden your horizons, then as a board member or as a senior management officer of your financial institution, you can provide the administrative leadership necessary for your institution to survive. One idea will be reiterated repeatedly throughout this book: Community financial institutions will survive. There may not be as many, they may come in different forms, and they may do different things by the year 2000 or 2010, but they will survive. They provide the financial leadership that is the backbone of the American community, state by state, and region by region. Community financial institutions will compete in an American banking industry with each other and with the national money center, even multinational banking organizations. There will be a place for both within the industry. In a recent article, John Buckman[1] said, "The community bank will survive because the money center bank will not run it out of business." Through people who are local in nature, the community bank will provide locally oriented services that cannot be met competitively by the intrastate and interstate bank holding company or branching system run by the money center and nationally oriented banks and thrifts. At the same time, competition in your local market may be such that to survive as a community bank, your organization must change completely and irrevocably. The fact that the community banking organization will survive as a prototype of delivery systems to a segment of the American economy does not guarantee your financial institution's survival. As you are quite aware, the life insurance actuarial tables indicate that only four out of 1,000 people will die at age 22. Have you noticed that they don't say which four people they are? It is just four people. You may be one of the four. The same thing is true with the survivability of the community bank/thrift. As a type of financial intermediary providing services to a segment of the American population, the community banking organization will survive. Your specific financial institution may not. This book is designed to make sure that you are one of the survivors, if you so desire. Breaking the mold of tradition is the first step on the road to survivability and success.

---

1. John A. Buckman, "Can Community Banks Survive?" *Business Law Today* (January/February 1996), pp. 44–51.

RECOMMENDATIONS

Eliminating tradition becomes the philosophical linchpin for your community financial institution. Follow the recommendations below to assist in breaking the mold and striking out anew:

- Whenever a decision must be made, think of new ways to do it.
- Retire and replace directors with new blood, if necessary to improve proactiveness and planning.
- Continue to retrain competent directors who see the future and work to get the financial institution into position for survival.
- Bring in senior management and staff from outside.
- Eliminate tradition through thinking proactively.
- Look forward to where your financial institution is going rather than where it has come from.

CHAPTER 2

What Is a Community Bank/Thrift?

Can It Survive?

What is a community bank/thrift? If you look it up in *Webster's* or *Funk & Wagnall*, you won't find any definition of community banking. You could even look it up in the encyclopedia of banking and still find no definition of community banking. The explanation is simple—no one has ever been able to adequately define a community bank/thrift. Let's look at a few attributes of community bank/thrifts as most of us have thought about them over the years:

- Small size.
- Not much sophistication.
- Uneducated personnel.
- In a rural area with buildings surrounded by cornfields.
- Very few branch offices.
- Simple services and not terribly complex technological products.
- Ownership by the board of directors—or at least a closely held group of investors.

Do not assume that these are negative qualities. Almost all of the above are indicative of a community bank/thrift—except for the "surrounded by cornfields" comment. Community bank/thrifts are small, located in rural areas in the main, provide simple services, have a small group of shareholders, and often have personnel that are less well-trained than staff at the bigger, metropolitan money center banks. On the other hand, several characteristics distinguish community banking favorably from its big city sisters and brothers:

- Knowledge of customers.
- Friendly, courteous service.
- Intimate knowledge of the community, its institutions, and its economy—and its foibles.
- Knowledge of character and creditworthiness of customers.
- Flexibility to meet customer needs without 100 pages of paperwork.
- All-out participation by staff and officers, as well as directors, in the community served by the bank.
- Strong links to economic development within areas served by the bank.
- Better products and services to people being served.

What is a community bank/thrift? It may be more a philosophy and/or a perception than it is a solid economic or financial statistic. It is true that it is almost impossible to be a community bank/thrift if you operate interstate and have a vast branching network filled with branch and assistant branch managers. Although some multibillion-dollar bank holding companies claim to be community banking operations, these types of institutions are really not. It is an oxymoron to utilize the term *community* in front of the term *multibank, interstate,* or *commercial bank holding company.* On the other hand, it is quite possible for a community banking organization to be more than $100 million or $200 million in assets. In fact, a community bank/thrift can operate with dozens of branches and still fall within the ambiance of being a community bank/thrift. What is important is neither size nor the number of offices, but the philosophy and management of the bank. If you think you are a community bank/thrift and act like a community bank/thrift, then you probably are a community bank/thrift.

What are the important ingredients or attributes that a community banker should have in order to operate as a community bank/thrift? These are relatively simple and certainly are not restricted by size, location, or number of offices:

- Be customer-oriented. The customer comes first, and the staff comes last.
- Price your products and services appropriately to produce stronger earnings, but don't gouge your customers—you need them.

- Operate your banking institution at hours that are favorable to your customers, not favorable to your staff.
- Provide products and services that are needed within your marketplace. Remain flexible and change products and services as demand indicates. Don't supply products and services simply because you are unwilling to change.
- Thank your customers all the time for their business—they have plenty of other alternatives. Utilizing your bank is the most important choice they can make.
- Remember that your shareholders are your owners and should be catered to at all times. If your investors are not loyal, your bank is doomed.
- Know your customers—a name is worth a thousand dollars.
- Remind your staff, your management, and your board of directors that you are a community bank/thrift and that the survivability of your community provides for the safe and solvent operation of your bank. Develop, expand, and maintain your community and you will prosper.
- Be concerned about what goes on in your market area—in terms of both people and condition. The community bank/thrift stands apart from megacenter banks in that it attempts to meet community needs first and, as a result, makes money—not vice versa.

Defining community banking is like capturing fog in a bottle or chasing a will of the wisp. A community bank/thrift looks a lot different than the neighboring bank down the road in the next state. The definition of your bank as a community bank/thrift depends more on your philosophy and how you operate the bank than it does on the number of offices or the size of your institution. If you keep your community in focus and remember that your customers come first (also remembering their first and last names, abilities, disabilities, achievements, and failures), then you will continue to be a strong community bank/thrift within your market.

RECOMMENDATIONS

- Community banking is a way of life, not necessarily defined by the size of the community financial institution.

- Promote, advertise, and sell your community bank as a community bank with roots to the local community at all times.
- Promote quality service and personal knowledge of your customers.
- Distinguish yourselves as a community financial institution.
- You may have 20 or 30 offices and you can still be a community bank. Just run them as if you only had one unit.
- Educate your staff and board of directors to promote yourself as a community financial institution. If you don't believe you are, your customers and your marketplace won't think you are.
- Be proactive within the community and be involved—you can't be a community banking financial institution with the wandering habits of a Methodist circuit rider.

CHAPTER 3

Visioning

The Importance of Strategic Planning for Survival

No, stop! Don't turn the page. This is not a chapter on how to strategic plan. By now you have been inundated by bank consultants like myself, trade associations, newsletters, books, and even the regulators telling you how to strategically plan your financial institution. This is not the reason why this chapter is number 3 on the techniques and procedures for how to survive as a community financial institution. I am not going to talk about *how* to strategic plan—I am going to talk about why you *must* strategically plan. There is a difference. We are not talking about conforming to regulators' demands for a "strategic plan" to be placed in the vault or on the shelf and then forgotten. This chapter discusses why it is essential to plan for the future of your financial institution in order to survive. We are not going to go into detail—if you want to do that, buy my book[1]—however, we are going to discuss the reasons why you should plan and then plan some more and then, on an annual basis, replan and replan so that you know where you are going as a banking institution.

VISIONING

Do you know where your financial institution is headed? Are you a member of the team that understands the big picture? Is your institution

---

1. Douglas V. Austin and Paul L. Simoff, *Strategic Planning for Banks: Meeting the Challenges of the 1990s*. Rolling Meadows: Bankers Publishing Company, 1990.

going to survive the next 10 to 15 years, or are you simply stacking up cord wood for the fireplace of life? If you as director or senior manager of a community banking financial institution do not know the answers to the above questions, then you won't survive. On the other hand, if you develop a corporate vision for your institution, and then implement that through solid strategic planning and operations, you will survive as a competitive, profitable, and solvent financial intermediary.

It is not uncommon to read in the financial press that community banking financial institutions don't plan, and therefore are subject to the vagaries of the marketplace and eventually death. I agree that some community banking financial institutions don't plan, but many do. We know that the big banks and thrifts do. In his book, *BottomLine Banking*[2] (co-authored with Larry Frieder and Robert Hedges), John B. McCoy, chairman and CEO of Bank One Corporation, discusses the importance of knowing where you are going, not just a few years ahead, but decades ahead. I am persuaded, and you probably also are as directors and managers, that Nations Bank, Bank of America, Chemical, and so on know where they wish to head in the years to come. They have developed a vision of what they are going to look like, where they are going to operate, what products and services they are going to provide, and with whom they are going to compete. Is this vision perfectly clear—20–20? Chances are, no, but it might be 20–40 and, with glasses, readily correctable. They have gone through the exercise of determining where they are going to be 10 and 20 years out. Have you?

Recently, I facilitated a strategic planning retreat at a 100-year-old bank that has never opened up a branch. The stockholders are old—Methuselah is a second cousin—and the bank holding company stock is closely held. In determining the "vision" for this bank, it became extremely obvious that it had no vision beyond that day of the retreat. Do you fall into this same pattern? Are you simply opening up in the morning, operating during the day, closing at night, and not paying attention to where you are going to be 10 years from now? Strategic planning doesn't bring you all the right answers, but it sure broadens your perspective as to what can be done, what should be done, and how to correct problems that currently plague your financial institution.

---

2. John B. McCoy, Larry A. Frieder, and Robert B. Hedges, Jr., *BottomLine Banking: Meeting the Challenges for Survival and Success.* Burr Ridge: Irwin Professional Publishing, 1994.

Visioning is the intellectual exercise of ascertaining the future course of the community banking financial institution 10 and 20 years out, and then attempting to strategically plan in increments of three to five years in order to reach the vision. Vision is a will of the wisp and will change over time as the banking industry changes. Economic and financial conditions fostered in the global marketplace will impact upon the vision and change it either suddenly or drastically as conditions fluctuate over time. However, you should not be discouraged as a board member or senior manager because you can't control such changes, but you certainly can control whether you are thinking about such changes within the market. You will be derelict in your duty if you simply operate the financial institution day-to-day. If you look around and determine that the board of directors has to be replaced because of age, the senior managers will be replaced because of age, the financial products and services will have to be changed because of competitive pressures, and the physical facilities will have to be changed due to obsolescence, then there is absolutely nothing to do in determining your vision for the next 20 years—ha ha! As I mentioned in Chapter 1, change is the only constant. There should be preplanning for conditions that are either eminent or possible. Visioning should be based upon what is not only practicable but realistic in the next 20 years. For example, at a recent strategic planning retreat, the president finally stood up and said, "My vision is that we should have branches throughout the upper lower portion of the lower peninsula of Michigan." At that time, the bank barely had branches 10 miles out of town. It shocked the rest of the directors who had no vision whatsoever that the president was thinking about a substantial one-third state presence. That is precisely the kind of thinking I want you to do. It is the kind of thinking that you as board members and senior managers have to do in order to determine how to survive as a community financial institution. Always remember that in case you are not doing this type of planning and thinking and visioning, your competitor across the street, down the road, in the next town, or across the state line may be doing such planning, and you are its target.

THE MISSION

There is a difference between a corporate vision and a corporate mission for your financial institution. The mission is more limited, is time-defined, and is characterized by a series of factual statements that outline salient characteristics of your bank or thrift. For example, you are an independent institution serving one county with a full range of products and services—hopefully high-quality—and you want an above-average rate of return on the investment of your shareholders.

The reason for a corporate mission is to place into one paragraph the elements and characteristics of your organization. Moreover, this mission could be promulgated to your customers, shareholders, and the community in general. It is a statement of what you are and what you plan to do. On the other hand, unlike the vision, it does not give away your long-term planning secrets, but simply explains what kind of an institution you are and what your emphasis happens to be at the current time and for the foreseeable future. The mission tells the public who you are, what you are, and where you plan to go, but at the same time doesn't give away all of the secrets that you have determined through your visioning and strategic planning. In essence, it gives the public half a loaf but doesn't give away your competitive secrets. The corporate mission should be reviewed annually by the board and senior management and revised as applicable since conditions within the market always change.

Finally, the mission tells your customers, shareholders, and the public whether you plan to remain independent or desire to sell. Almost a decade ago, one of my clients developed a strategic planning mission that said that they were positioning themselves to sell within three years. Can you guess how long it took before the phone rang after this was distributed? This was a sneaky but effective way to let the public know that they were interested in selling, and the institution did sell at a very good price shortly thereafter. On the other hand, tell everybody you don't want to sell, and perhaps the speculative fever in your stock will go away and you will have more comfort with the loyal shareholders remaining.

GOALS AND OBJECTIVES

Strategic plans revolve around goal and objective setting. These goals and objectives are both financial and nonfinancial in nature. There are certain characteristics that the directors and managers should realize at the time these goals are set:

- All goals and objectives should be realistically attainable.
- All goals and objectives should be realistic vis-à-vis banking standards of the industry.

- Goals and objectives should be attainable over time, not overnight.
- Financial goals may be ranges and may not be increased annually if high performance has already been achieved.
- Nonfinancial goals and objectives are different from bank to bank and thrift to thrift.

The most important element of strategic planning is to make sure that the goals and objectives you set for yourself are realistically attainable by the management. Since most board members have no clue how to run a community banking institution, approving goals and objectives that are unattainable by your management is a self-defeating exercise. Obviously you want to do as well as peer group banks or thrifts, or even better. Thus, the Uniform Bank Performance Report and its thrift counterpart make a good benchmark for analysis. If you as board members want your management to earn a 1.6 percent rate of return on average assets and the peer group is only earning .9 percent then the 1.6 percent rate of return on average assets is probably unrealistic, unattainable, and unfair. On the other hand, if the management says they can't earn more than a .9 percent rate of return on average assets and the peer group is earning 1.6 percent, then strong consideration should be given to replacing management since they obviously are underachievers. Utilize the Uniform Bank Performance Report, functional cost analysis, and other financial ratio tabulations in order to assist yourself in setting goals and objectives that are realistically attainable by your management, thus providing safety and solvency for your shareholders, customers, and employees.

The second most important element in determining goals and objectives is to ascertain appropriate timing for such achievement. You can't jump your rate of return on average assets from .6 in 1996 to 1.8 percent in 1997. This is fundamentally impossible to do unless you cashier 50 percent of your employees. It is important for the board of directors and senior management to work together to determine the timing for achievement of such goals and objectives, whether they be financial or nonfinancial. Once the timing has been determined, agreed upon, and set forth in the strategic plan, then senior management should be held accountable on reaching such goals and objectives within the timeframe determined. Lack of achievement is tantamount to dismissal or at least strong censure by the board. Since community banking financial institutions are not charities, goals and objectives should be reached, or consequences should be faced by the senior management who has failed to reach them. Your institution will only survive if it is highly tuned, profitable, and/or capitally adequate. Failure to reach your goals and objectives will adversely affect your ability to survive as a community banking financial institution.

Too often the board of directors demands that the senior management always increase the financial performance of the institution. In fact, I used to talk that way also. In my first couple of books on strategic planning I thought it was necessary for the bank or thrift to improve year after year, year after year, ad nauseam. I am now older and perhaps wiser. Today, if you have a high-performance bank or thrift that is outperforming the peer group, don't demand even more—just accept your outstanding position currently. For example, if you are earning a 1.5 rate of return on average assets while everybody around you is earning 1.2, just be happy with the 1.5 year after year and don't try to get 1.75, which is unattainable long-term. As board members you should realize how difficult it is to maintain solid performance. If you are a high-performance bank or thrift that is far above competitors within your marketplace, reward your management with stock options, salary increases, and employment contracts, and keep them in town. They are your first line of defense.

ACTION IMPLEMENTATION PLANS

The most important implementation technique is to prioritize the goals and objectives set forth above. The biggest mistake you can make as a board of directors is to demand that your senior management simultaneously implement all of the goals and objectives that you have set forth. Let me give you an example: I was reading the strategic plan of a $200 million community bank in Michigan and noted that it had formed 14 task forces to implement the action plans set forth in the strategic plan. Since the vice president for operation was a former student of mine, I called and asked how things were going. I had noted that of the 14 task forces, he was chairman of seven and was a member of four others. He told me that the 11 task forces were doing just fine, but he hadn't been in his office doing his regular work for six weeks. I rest my case. You cannot continue to function as a financial institution if you load down your overworked senior management and staff with strategic planning implementation programs so that they can't do their jobs. Let's assume that you end up with 13 financial and nonfinancial goals and objectives. Of these 13, you want to do 10 next year and the other 3 over the next several years thereafter. Realistically, you won't get the 10 done. You are far better off picking 4 for next year, 5 for the second year, and 4 for the third year, covering all 13 of the priorities. At the end of this year, then rearrange your priorities for the years to come. You can achieve 4 or 5 action plans—you cannot achieve all of them. Your staff still has to continue to operate on a day-to-day basis. If you had excess time for these people now, you probably would get rid of one or two of them.

Financial goals and objectives can only be implemented through concrete action plans. As noted above, prioritization of these plans is essential. Moreover, review of the implementation is also crucial. Your board is the supervisor and monitor of your financial institution. If you assign work to be done by the senior management and delegate to staff, then such implementation should be reviewed by you on a regular basis. Thus, the board and the senior management should work out the timing of implementing each of the strategic action plans as outlined by the strategic plan itself, and the senior management should be held accountable to the board for such implementation. There may be perfectly good reasons why sometimes the implementation won't take place on time—and the board of directors should be cognizant of these reasons—but the senior management should be under pressure to make sure that the implementation is achieved within the framework approved. Obviously, if you have too many action plans going forth at the same time, then you may not be able to implement all of them, if any.

REPLANNING

In 1990, when I gave one of my strategic planning speeches to a board of directors seminar in Iowa, I found that only three banks out of 93 had a strategic plan in written form. Five years later when I gave the same type of strategic planning program to the Independent Bankers Association of Texas (IBAT) I discovered that over 75 percent of the banks in the audience already had a written strategic plan. However, there was, and still is, a problem concerning strategic planning by community banking organizations. When I asked the IBAT members how many of them had reviewed their strategic plan the previous year, I got a much smaller percentage of yes answers.

Let me give you another example: Last year I called one of my Indiana community bank clients where I had done the original strategic plan. I called soliciting business to see whether he wanted me to do a strategic planning retreat for him. His answer was, "No, it was a three-year plan and we are only in the second year of the plan so we won't need to see you until two years from now." Obviously, something got lost in the translation. Every year is a planning year at your bank or thrift. Every year you must do a replanning of your strategic plan. You do not have a five-year economic plan like the Soviets did. Parenthetically, you know how well the Soviet economy did with its so-called five-year plan. Every year is a new planning period and each year you should review your strategic plan.

Planning is an ongoing exercise. The strategic plan is a living, dynamic organism. The worst thing you can do is to approve the strategic plan and then place it on the shelf or in the bank vault. Replanning becomes second nature to you year after year if you include it within your annual regular duties as a board of directors or senior management. So far the most imposing task is the first strategic plan. As you review the strategic plan year after year, there will be minor changes and changes of direction, not massive mountains of work to be done with your initial strategic plan. However, it should be reviewed and changed as necessary each year in order to keep current with the trends within the industry and beyond.

THE STRATEGIC PLANNING RETREAT

The most efficient way to strategically plan year after year is at a strategic planning retreat. This retreat should be held off-premises. If you are off-premises—whether you are at a local motel, a resort, or imposing city panorama—you are away from the telephone and interruptions. The strategic planning retreat allows your board and senior management to provide time and resources necessary to review the plan and make the necessary changes thereto. If you attempt to hold the planning session at your bank/thrift, the phone rings, the staff needs help, and, more importantly, the directors are interrupted by their own business/social contacts and situations. You can concentrate more fully and actually achieve a more efficient strategic planning review and reimplementation if it is handled through a strategic planning retreat. Furthermore, and this is not unimportant, you can make the strategic planning retreat be a social as well as a business event. Often the board of directors doesn't know whether the senior management can chew gum and talk at the same time, and the senior management feels remote and inaccessible to the board or vice versa. The strategic planning retreat provides directors, managers, and spouses with a social interaction that in the long run *may* improve the overall efficiency of the board–management relationship. Notice that I said *may*—I certainly can't guarantee that it will since you might actually find out you don't like the management very well. However, I have never run across that in any of my strategic planning retreats and I find that the senior management (other than the CEO) finds the interaction very worthwhile since they get to know more about the board members and their spouses. Finally, it should be noted that the board of directors may have to either replace or, in the long run, promote some of the other senior managers after the current president/CEO is gone. The more the board members know about the junior and senior managers, the better off the institution is. A strategic planning retreat has no liabilities, just assets, and should be utilized on an annual basis as an educational device for reviewing, revising, and reapproving the strategic plan.

As mentioned in an earlier chapter, it is necessary to break tradition, understand change, and be aware of the moving trends within and outside the industry. The value of an outside facilitator at your strategic planning retreat is critical. At least once every two years, or perhaps only once every three years, you should have your strategic planning retreat run by an outside facilitator. If you use an outside facilitator, he or she can provide you with a global perspective concerning your community banking institution. You as board members may not have ever been a board member of another financial institution. You as senior management may have only worked for this institution. Your facilitator has been a consultant to tens, if not hundreds, of financial institutions. He will have performed strategic planning retreat facilitations for many banks and thrifts. He can assist you in breaking tradition, understanding change, and developing goals and objectives that can be implemented realistically at your institution. Furthermore, he can be constructively critical as to the current financial condition and performance of your institution, comment on the management strength and board of directors quality, and assist you in determining which direction to go and how to get there. You don't have to utilize these outside facilitators every year—your chairman can handle it every other year or for two years out of three. However, once you bring the outside facilitator in, you can get a perspective of what is going on far beyond your own board room and this will assist you in determining how best to plan your institution into the future. The outside facilitator's cost is minimal and the reward is great.

WHO'S RESPONSIBLE FOR THE STRATEGIC PLAN?

As author of over 200 strategic plans, I find that one of the most interesting facets I run across is who is responsible for the strategic plan. At some financial institutions, the board of directors runs the strategic planning process. They include only the president/CEO, who is on the board. At other institutions, the management prepares the strategic plan and the board of directors signs off on the plan. There is a third way—the board of directors does nothing. Unfortunately, I have run across that too many times recently where the management has to do all the work and the board of directors does not want to be involved at all. That is not the way to survive as a financial institution. The leadership has to come from the board, not from the management. Finally, there are few cases where the board of directors and the management of all the department heads get together to do the strategic planning. That's OK, but many of the department heads are not capable of seeing the big picture, and results are usually inconsistent. As an outside consultant, I have spent many a day preparing strategic plans put together from the bottom up, since inconsistent nature, experience, and expertise of the department heads will result in developing a camel rather than a horse. Once the strategic plan has been adopted (or revised, depending upon your situation), senior management should review the strategic plan with the department heads and have the strategic plans of each department or function within your institution develop from the overall plan (i.e., plan from the top down rather than from the bottom up). As the department heads become more expert in developing functional strategic plans, you may be able to, over time, include them in the planning process and improve the rate of the strategic planning technically more quickly.

WHAT THE STRATEGIC PLAN SHOULD LOOK LIKE

As a final comment, let me explain that the strategic plan for your financial institution does not have to be 100 pages long. Often when I talk to boards of directors, they think they are developing the Magna Carta or, even worse, that they are writing *War and Peace* by Tolstoy. Initially, your strategic plan should be only as long as necessary to cover the subject. That may be 10 to 20 pages. It should cover current economic and financial conditions within your marketplace, the current situation within your bank (called the "situation analysis"), definitions of the vision and mission for your financial institution, and then expositions on the financial and nonfinancial goals and objectives followed by the strategic action implementation plans. For the first several years, this will be a relatively short document. As you strategically plan year after year, and your board and senior management as well as department heads become more proficient, the strategic plan will expand automatically. In essence, you learn to crawl first, then walk, and finally run the marathon in strategic planning. Do not be ashamed that your first strategic plan is only 20 pages. That is 20 pages more than you had the year before, and it's in writing, you have approved it, and you should follow it.

RECOMMENDATIONS

- If you don't have a strategic plan, develop one.
- If you have a strategic plan, review and revise it annually.
- Utilize a strategic planning retreat to plan your financial institution's activities.
- Your strategic plan must be realistic and attainable; if not, your financial institution will not survive.
- Hold your senior management accountable for meeting the strategic action plan implementation schedules.
- Prioritize the strategic action plan implementation so as not to overburden your senior management and adversely impact their achievement.
- Utilize the strategic plan as a senior management review performance tool.
- Review your strategic plan and goals and objectives vis-à-vis peer group financial institutions. Do not expect miracles. You can realistically expect above-average performance.
- Utilize an outside strategic planning facilitator at your retreat. An outside global perspective is good for you and your strategic plan.
- The strategic planning process is your number one priority for the entire year as a board member. The other duties you have fall below concern for long-term survivability.
- If you haven't developed a vision, your financial institution will be going nowhere. Make sure you have a vision of your financial institution within your marketplace for the next 20 years.

CHAPTER 4

Bank and Thrift Holding Companies

Keys to Flexibility

Bank and thrift holding companies are here to stay. As of year end 1994 there were 817 multibank holding companies operating throughout the United States as well as 69 multithrift holding companies. However, these are not the figures of our interest. As of the same date, there were 4,462 one-bank holding companies and 599 unitary thrift holding companies operating in the United States. These *are* the holding companies of our interest in this chapter. At the same time, there were 3,700 commercial banks still operating without bank holding companies and 770 thrifts operating without holding companies. This chapter is essentially designed to assist those of you who are not in holding companies to understand why the holding company format is of value to you as a survival technique for a community bank/thrift.

If you are not a bank/thrift holding company, read this chapter and understand the reasons why the holding company format will be of assistance to you. If you are a bank/thrift holding company, review this chapter simply to make sure that you are taking advantage of all of the types of nonbanking activities available to you, and thus utilize this chapter as a review of your current holding company philosophy.

GENERAL CONCEPT

The holding company is a corporate device by which the bank/thrift is owned by a state-chartered corporation. The reason for reorganizing your bank/thrift into a holding company subsidiary is to provide increased flexibility as to corporate opportunities available to your bank/thrift. In most political jurisdictions in the United States, commercial banks and thrifts have more limited corporate powers than do regular corporations. The holding company is a regular corporation chartered either in your state or in a foreign state (such as Delaware), and provides increased corporate powers and flexibility over your commercial bank/thrift. In an increasingly competitive marketplace, flexibility provides the community banking financial institution with new expanded corporate powers that will assist the bank/thrift in meeting competitive needs within the marketplace and thus provide a better chance for community bank/thrift survival.

This chapter does not discuss how to form a holding company. That is unimportant to us in this book. Countless competent professional firms in the marketplace can assist you in forming a holding company. If you are interested in doing so, contact several of them, have them provide you with a proposal, interview them, and check out their references. The cost of forming a bank or thrift holding company will be in the neighborhood of $25,000 to $50,000, but that cost may be infinitesimal vis-à-vis the benefits received by such formation. Too often the board of directors may look simply at the cost, consider it too high, and thus not form the holding company. On the other hand, if formation of the holding company permits you to control your shareholder base, shift from older shareholders to newer shareholders, stop unsolicited takeovers by corporate raiders, and provide you with the flexibility of new corporate powers, then the benefits of the holding company format may overwhelm any minor financial costs incurred in the formation of the holding company. For example, a simple trick is to expense the holding company formation over two years. Furthermore, most of the capitalized costs may be amortized over five years. Thus, the actual expenses of forming the holding company are not a burden on any one year's financial statements. Moreover, the holding company format provides your senior management with opportunities to enter new lines of business and to become more competitive within your marketplace, thus increasing profitability and improving your chances of survival.

PROTECTING YOURSELF FROM TAKEOVER

One of the most important reasons for utilizing the holding company is to provide, within the articles of incorporation and the bylaws of the holding company, antitakeover measures that limit the opportunities for outside groups to take over your financial institution. Most community banks and thrifts, as banks and thrifts, cannot provide antitakeover measures within their state or federal charters and/or bylaws. However, as a wholly owned subsidiary of a bank/thrift holding company, the holding company's incorporation clauses and/or bylaws may contain strong antitakeover measures that prevent the bank or thrift from being sold to an unwanted attacker. These antitakeover measures—such as a fair-price provision, a supermajority clause forcing the attacker to meet a higher standard than the state or federal merger/acquisition percentage, poison pills, and residency clauses—provide for continuity assurance at your financial institution. You do not have to be concerned about an unwanted takeover. It should be noted that these antitakeover measures work in your favor if the unsolicited bid is not desired by your board of directors. On the other hand, these antitakeover measures are not operative if your board of directors is in favor of a merger/acquisition with another party. If your vision is to remain independent, you may not be able to guarantee it 100 percent, but you can protect that goal if you have a holding company with strong antitakeover measures. You could assume that having a closely held bank or thrift would provide you with such assurances, but what happens if several of your major shareholders pass away and the stock becomes available in the marketplace in order to settle their estates? If you do not have antitakeover measures at the holding company level, your community banking institution is available for sale (i.e., it is up for play).

REDEMPTION OF CORPORATE STOCK

Almost every commercial bank or thrift is not legally permitted to repurchase its own outstanding securities. Several states, like Ohio, permit such redemption after a redemption request is approved by the state regulatory authority. If you have a bank or thrift holding company, you can redeem your corporate securities on a regular basis, often without any regulatory approval of any kind. For example, a bank holding company regulated and supervised by the Federal Reserve System may purchase up to 10 percent of its outstanding shares (measured by value) on an annual basis without permission by the Federal Reserve System. Parenthetically, I should note that if such a transaction would be financially imprudent, results of such a purchase will be frowned upon by the Federal Reserve System. If you desire to buy back more than 10 percent of your stock, then you simply ask for approval from the Federal Reserve System. Thus, if a major shareholder owning 15 percent of the stock dies, you have the ability to repurchase the stock and place it into treasury and thus control the outstanding stock that would have been placed on the market by such maneuver. This is not a legal treatise, so do not assume that you can resell these securities back into the marketplace without consulting your legal counsel. If you resell these securities, you may be violating SEC rules and regulations and/or blue sky laws.

The ability to redeem your corporate stock as a bank or thrift holding company is the most important reason why holding companies have been formed over the past 20 years in the community banking industry. There are no national statistics available on how old the average shareholder is in the community banking/thrift industry, but just look around your board and think about your shareholder base. It has now been over 60 years since the banking industry was reorganized after the Banking Holiday of 1933. For many of the commercial banks and thrifts that were reorganized during the Depression, original shareholders either have passed away and bequeathed their securities to younger members of the family or else now have the physical appearance of the witches from *Macbeth* as they totter to and from the bank/thrift on their canes or maneuver in their wheelchairs. Your financial institution may have a loaded timebomb in the shareholder base. Thus the corporate redemption policy is essential so that you can offer a market to your shareholders if and when they need it. As will be discussed in greater detail in Chapter 5, control of your shareholder base may determine your survivability quotient. More banks and thrifts are sold by shareholders who desire liquidity at a fair price than financial institutions that fail. You may have an outstanding financial condition, have a history of profitable financial performance and be more than adequately capitalized, but if your owners want cash, and all they have today is an illiquid, unmarketable security, you will probably be sold unless you can develop an alternative technique. The holding company is the vehicle to provide that alternative for you.

EXPANDED PRODUCTS AND SERVICES THROUGH CORPORATE POWERS

In general, bank holding companies are able to increase their products and services through nonbanking subsidiaries in greater amount than either national or state banks. I realize that is a gross generalization and subject to the type of bank or thrift charter you have as well as the powers currently available at the bank/thrift level—and it may change over the next five years. However, 4(c)(8) activities and the thrift equivalent provide for nonbanking subsidiary activities greater than the average bank or thrift can offer.

Table 4–1 shows the "community" nonbanking activities available as of January 1996 for Federal Reserve registered bank holding companies under Section 4(c)(8) activities. These activities can all be provided to the customers of the bank subsidiary through nonbank affiliates of the holding company. These are corporate subsidiaries separate and distinct from the commercial bank subsidiary, all owned 100 percent by the bank holding company. Although some of these may be offered by the commercial bank subsidiary itself, if they are so provided by the bank subsidiary, they can only be provided through the offices of the bank based upon the banking restrictions of the commercial bank. If the same services and products are provided by the nonbanking subsidiaries of the holding company, they can be provided internationally. There is no geographic branching restriction on where the offices of the nonbanking subsidiary of the holding company can be located. For example, the money center, multibank holding companies provide consumer finance subsidiary activities throughout the United States, although until recently most commercial bank subsidiaries have been able to operate only within one state or else interstate through bank holding company subsidiaries. As interstate branching becomes available over the next decade, many of these consumer finance offices may be spun into the commercial bank branches located throughout the country, but currently nonbanking subsidiaries such as leasing companies, consumer finance companies, factors, and trust companies operate nationally from banks that for all intents and purposes have their depository gathering powers only within one state or several states. In the case of the community bank holding company, the purpose of the nonbanking subsidiary is to provide the same products and services outside the commercial bank and perhaps in locations where the commercial bank has not yet decided to branch or is incapable by law of doing so.

In your community, in reference to Table 4–1, you may be able to provide financial planning services, investment management services, leasing services, factoring services, credit bureau services, tax preparation services, and so on, all of which are performed through nonbanking subsidiary corporate affiliates of your bank holding company. Furthermore, these offices do not have to be within your commercial bank/thrift; they can be located in distant communities no

TABLE 4-1

Community Bank *Selected* Activity Alternatives under Section Y-4(c)(8)
of the Bank Holding Act of 1956

Mortgage banking
Consumer finance
Investment and financial advising
Full-payout leasing of personal or real property
Providing bookkeeping or data processing services
Underwriting credit life, accident, and health insurance
Providing courier services
Sale of money orders, travelers' checks, and savings bonds
Discount brokerage of securities
Tax preparation and planning
Operating a collection agency
Operating a credit bureau
Appraisals of personal property
Check guarantee and verification services
Operating a distressed or healthy savings and loan association
Performing appraisals, advising, and brokerage of commercial real estate properties
Providing community development advisory and related services

differently than the old loan production office. Whether you utilize such
product and service delivery vehicles depends upon your marketplace and
what is demanded, but the holding company format provides such ability
and in many cases your commercial bank charter does not.

BORROWING FLEXIBILITY

In most jurisdictions, it is easier to borrow at the holding company level
than it is at the bank level. Why would a commercial bank or thrift decide
to borrow funds? The reason is simple—it needs the funds for some
legitimate corporate purpose. For example, if you need to buy back $1
million of your own stock, and you don't want to take the funds out of
capital directly, then borrow $1 million from an institutional investor, an
independent banker's bank, or a correspondent bank, place it into the
liabilities of your bank holding company, and redeem the stock. Then you
can utilize dividends from the banking subsidiary which are upstreamed to
the holding company to repay the outstanding loan from an institutional
source. In many state jurisdictions, commercial banks cannot borrow in
such a manner at the bank level itself. The borrowing ability at the holding
company is increased flexibility. Another reason would be to fund a

leveraged ESOP program, which would redeem outstanding stock or fund treasury stock or newly authorized stock, or you might borrow for purposes of purchasing branches from other banks or thrifts within your marketplace, or utilize the borrowings as a part of the purchase for cash of another financial institution. Although such borrowings will have an adverse effect upon the consolidated tangible capital of your holding company, borrowings at the holding company level will leave the capital of your bank at the same level, which is favorable when assessed by state and federal regulatory agencies. All such borrowings must be approved by the Federal Reserve System or, in the alternative, under circumstances by the state banking department, the comptroller of the currency, the FDIC, or the OTS, and the borrowings must be financially prudent and within the constraints outlined by the regulatory authorities. However, establishment of standby lines of credit for such borrowing purposes may be advantageous to the quick, efficient corporate maneuvers when (1) branch and/or financial institution purchases become available (2) there is a need to redeem outstanding stock from a shareholder's estate almost instantaneously.

Borrowing is also available for an emergency infusion of capital at the bank level through original borrowings at the holding company level in case you run into a significant loan charge-off problem. If necessary, you could borrow at the holding company level and downstream the capital to the bank for purposes of replenishing capital charged off by significant loan losses. This is rarely utilized, but does provide another mechanism for achieving survivability if such an adverse scenario takes place.

RECOMMENDATIONS

- If you need to buy back corporate stock from older shareholders, form a holding company.
- If you have a need for expanded services within your community, form a holding company.
- If you need to have offices beyond your commercial bank/thrift offices, form a holding company.
- If you need to borrow for corporate purposes, form a holding company.
- If none of these needs applies to your financial institution, do not form a holding company. There should be a legitimate, corporate, business purpose before spending the money.
- Plan ahead. It is better to have the holding company in place than be pressured into scrambling in an emergency!

CHAPTER 5

Shareholder Relations

If You Do Not Control Your Shareholders, You Will Not Survive

The most common reason for the sale of banks and thrifts is because the shareholders want liquidity, and the only way they can transform their illiquid, unmarketable millstone of a corporate security into cash is to sell the community banking institution. If you, as a member of the board of directors or senior management, want to survive as an independent community banking institution, you must provide an alternative vehicle for your shareholders when they wish to sell. As noted in Chapter 4, the shareholder base of the community banking industry is predominantly old or has already transferred stock into second- and third-generation hands that are no longer loyal to your institution. Thus, you have a loaded time bomb in your stockholder list that can force you to sell your institution even though it is operating profitably, has more than adequate capital, and has an outstanding future within your community.

This chapter outlines techniques by which you as the board of directors and senior management can control your shareholder base so as to provide liquidity for your stock, maintain a "fair market value" for your securities, and maintain loyalty from your shareholders during periods of strength and weakness so as to mitigate the shareholders' influence on the survivability quotient. If you, as a board, are interested in selling, then obviously this chapter will be of little value to you. On the other hand, if you wish to remain independent and have a vision of where your institution can go over the next 10 to 20 years, you must make sure that the shareholder base does not become the largest stumbling block to the success of your plans. If your shareholders want liquidity and have no alternative other than to sell the institution, you have not succeeded in providing the necessary vehicles for transferring current shareholders to new shareholders, and thus you will not succeed in your vision of remaining an independent community bank or thrift institution.

This chapter has a somewhat limited scope. For those of you reading this book who are in mutual organizations, this chapter will be of no intrinsic value to you. However, this is the only chapter that does not apply directly to you, and if you decide to convert from a mutual form of structure to a stock format, then this chapter automatically applies. Therefore, you can learn something by skimming this chapter rather than simply avoiding it—perhaps in the next several years, this chapter will become relevant to you.

NATURE OF SHAREHOLDERS

It is crucial to understand that your shareholders are investors. They may have invested one week ago or 10 years ago, or (in the case of many of your shareholders) they may have received the stock as bequests from their parents or grandparents who purchased the stock as much as 50 or 100 years ago. Shareholders are investors, and they are far less loyal than they were years ago. They want (expect) a favorable rate of return, and when they want to sell, they want to sell! The worst thing you can have is a restless shareholder base. Moreover, there may be a select number of shareholders who have such a significant percentage of your stock that easy disposal of the stock is impossible. These shareholders— most of whom I would call affiliated parties—may have enough stock to cause you considerable difficulties if it all became available on the market at the same time, and thus became available to an interested purchaser. Furthermore, if it became available on the market and you could not sell it, then the supply overhanging the market would have an adverse impact on the market value of your securities. You should be extremely interested in making sure that your significant shareholders have more than one mechanism for disposing of their securities in your financial institution whenever they want at a fair market value. If you provide this, your shareholders will not be a rebellious thorn in your corporate side.

JUST THE FACTS, MA'AM, JUST THE FACTS

As board members, you should understand the following facts about your shareholders:

- They are not as loyal as they used to be.
- They want cash, they want cash, and they want cash.
- They do not care to whom they sell their securities.
- They want a fair market value, not a depressed arbitrary price.
- When they want to sell, they want to sell now—not six months later.
- If you provide them with methods by which they can sell either to you or in the open market, they will be placated.
- Most community banks/thrifts do not have an organized securities market.
- Less than 10 percent of the community banks/thrifts have any investment banker "making a market" for their securities.
- Most community banks/thrifts trade at an unreasonably low market value that is nowhere close to "fair market value."
- If you operate as a commercial bank/thrift and do not have a holding company, you cannot repurchase stock.
- If you operate in a holding company format, you can redeem the corporate stock, thus permitting a vehicle for liquidity to your shareholders.

It really does not make any difference whether you have 50 shareholders or 500 shareholders. If they want to sell, they want to sell. It is obvious that if you have only 50 shareholders, then there will be larger blocks of stock outstanding. On the other hand, if you have 500 shareholders, you may be able to sell the smaller blocks of stock throughout the community better. Again, that will depend upon whether you have an investment banker making a market for you. Since less than 10 percent of all community banking organizations have an investment banker making a market, you should provide the vehicle for such purchase. As explained extensively in Chapter 4, the bank/thrift holding company becomes the vehicle for such repurchase.

It only makes common sense to provide yourself with the most flexibility possible. If you can keep your shareholders placated by having the vehicles necessary to buy their stock out when they so desire, then your chances of surviving as a community institution are far greater.

UNDERSTANDING YOUR SHAREHOLDERS LIST

The first thing I recommend to boards of directors is to survey, in depth, your shareholders list. Analyze that list as to the name, age, health, and location of your shareholders. If your shareholders are aged, living in a local nursing home, or located 1,500 miles away from your home community, you have a potential problem. Then, if you superimpose the number of shares they have on top of the previous matrix, it can become an almost insurmountable problem unless you have a corporate stock repurchase vehicle available. The second step is to go out and talk to your shareholders. I don't mean all your shareholders, just the ones who have plenty of stock. For example, you should contact every shareholder who has more than 5 percent of your stock. In fact, if you are a widely held community bank/thrift, you might want to bring that percentage down to 2 percent or 3 percent. You want to go out and talk to them and find out what they plan to do with their stock when they pass away—even though this sounds morbid, you as a community bank/thrift are trying to figure out how their investment will impinge upon your survivability. If you have established a corporate stock redemption policy at the holding company level, you can inform the shareholders that there is a second vehicle available in case they need the liquidity at the time of their demise. Furthermore, you could even enter into a buy/sell agreement or first right of refusal agreement to repurchase their stock at the time it hits their estate. The only caveat here is that you must have the financial resources available at that time (i.e., the repurchase of their stocks must be a prudent decision under the Business Judgment Rule as it impacts upon the actions of the board of directors). Thus, if your financial institution has the capital adequacy, strength of profitability, and substantial ability to borrow at the holding company level, you can make such agreements with your major shareholders in order to provide a shareholder transition. On the other hand, if your shareholders decide to bequeath their stock to heirs and descendants, this problem is ameliorated.

After you have analyzed your entire shareholder base, then the board of directors can decide whether you have a significant long-term transitional problem within your shareholder base, or whether several shareholders shifting their stock to descendants or selling such stock will solve your problem. This survey should be done no less than every three years. Analyze your shareholders list about every three months, internally, to determine whether there are people purchasing your stock either directly or through nominees who may cause you a problem in the long run. Today, especially in the thrift industry, there are voracious speculators within every thrift shareholder base, individuals who have no interest whatsoever in the long-term performance of the thrift, but who are interested in a quick sale of the institution in order to double or triple their investment.

CORPORATE STOCK REDEMPTION POLICY

Table 5–1 is an illustrative corporate stock redemption policy that you could modify for your community banking organization. This policy, passed by the board of directors and reaffirmed on an annual basis, permits you to repurchase the corporate stock as long as you have the financial resources to do so, and in doing so, the decision by the board would be financially prudent. I note these caveats seriously, since repurchase of corporate stock when your capital account is inadequate will bring down the wrath of the state and federal banking regulators on your back. Thus, the corporate stock redemption policy is conditional on your financial condition and performance. This is the best we can do, but it may be far better than where you are today. It does permit you to repurchase the securities if you have the capability.

FINDING CAPITAL FOR REDEMPTION

Community banking organizations, such as your local bank/thrift, have higher capital levels (regardless of how it is measured) than do the money center banks. At the time of the writing of this book, we have seen five straight years of record commercial bank profits, even though surviving thrifts are increasing profitability year to year. Capital levels are at historical highs as we begin the second half of the decade of the 90s, while the remaining thrift institutions have also recovered in terms of profitability, although we have not hit historical highs due to the significant downsizing of the industry. Your financial institution is probably more than adequate capitally. If your capital to asset ratio is 200 basis points higher than your peer group's, you are significantly capitalized. However, if you need to redeem corporate stock within the next five years, this excess capital may not be enough.

A survey of your shareholders may indicate that you must raise $1 million, $2 million, or even $3 million in cash in order to redeem the

TABLE 5-1

Illustrative Bank Holding Company Stock Redemption Policy

To be approved by the board of directors of
[name of bank holding company]
on _____, 1996

The board of directors of **[name of bank holding company]**, acting in their capacity as directors of said holding company, during a regular meeting of the board of directors, hereby approves and adopts the following bank holding company stock redemption policy utilized by **[name of bank holding company]** until either repealed or modified by the board of directors at a future date:

The **[name of bank holding company]** board of directors hereby resolve to purchase Company's common stock from time to time within the restrictions of the Federal Reserve Act and at a fair value. **[name of bank holding company]** shall only purchase common shares for either Treasury stock purposes or for retirement, based upon advice of legal counsel, and after approval by the board of directors.

In order for an objective fair value to be determined, **[name of bank holding company]** shall engage an objective third-party valuation expert firm for purposes of determining fair value of the stock for repurchase purposes, on an annual basis, or whenever appropriate under the Business Judgment Rule. The valuation shall be relied upon by the board of directors in determining the price to repurchase the Company's stock from time to time.

[name of bank holding company] shall not purchase the common stock of Company unless it has the financial resources to do so, and it is the opinion of the board of directors that the Company's financial condition would not be impaired by such purchase. The board of directors does not have to purchase stock offered to it by its shareholders, but may, at its discretion based upon its fulfilling its duty of care, purchase such stock if it is legally and financially appropriate.

The Company shall have the discretion to purchase stock from individual shareholders without requesting to repurchase stock from all shareholders. The board of directors of **[name of bank holding company]** and its delegated officers shall repurchase on behalf of the Company, shares offered to it by the shareholders without pro rata purchase from all shareholders, and may for legitimate business purposes purchase none or all of the shares of any individual shareholder. The board of directors shall inform the shareholders of this discretionary mode of repurchase so that all shareholders know that they may or may not have their shares repurchased during any calendar period. The board of directors shall do everything in its power to repurchase any shares from its shareholders that are requested to be purchased, but cannot guarantee that they will do so, unless all financial and legal conditions are met, and that it is an appropriate activity of the holding company to undertake based upon the board of directors fulfilling its duty of care, via the Business Judgment Rule.

corporate securities that will become available over the next 5 to 10 years. Thus, one of your corporate purposes as a board of directors is to stockpile capital, either at the bank level or at the holding company level, for purposes of redeeming the securities. In this particular circumstance, you cannot have too much capital. Furthermore, you must consider that the securities will be repurchased at a "fair market value" that could be significantly above book value per share. Thus, the amount of stock necessary for your survival as an ongoing community banking institution may be 50 percent or more greater than the book value per share of the shares redeemed. The alternative is to sell. If that is not what you want to do, then you had better have a program available for implementation whenever it becomes necessary as your shareholders desire and/or demand redemption of their corporate securities.

It will be necessary for you to determine what will be adequate capital after you have redeemed the securities. Furthermore, chances are you cannot predict when the securities will be redeemed, and thus you should err on the conservative side. As community banks/thrifts, you should not be concerned about the rate of return on equity as much as being concerned about the rate of return on assets. If your vision is to remain an independent bank serving your market area for the next 20 years, it will be more important to transfer those shareholders who wish to become liquid into new shareholders than it will be to have a particular rate of return on equity.

If your survey indicates that there is a measurable amount of redemption expected, but not in the millions of dollars, then the ability to borrow at the holding company level will become the most feasible way to redeem the securities. If you are widely held, the best solution for handling the corporate redemption is to provide a liquid market through a regional investment banking house that will provide a true, organized market for your securities.

LOOKING FOR NEW INVESTORS

As your current shareholders mature (which is a euphemism for aging and dying off or retiring to Florida or Arizona), you need to replace your current shareholders with newer shareholders within the market served by your financial institution. There is a tendency for boards of directors to get so involved in the quality of assets or the past due loan ratios that they fail to understand that the community bank/thrift needs a strong shareholder base within the market to provide the foundation for continued independence and service. As your shareholders mature, you must replace them with new shareholders. Thus, the new shareholders must be given an incentive to purchase the securities, and you should provide programs to transfer the shares from the current shareholders to new shareholders. If you have an active, liquid market, you will not need to redeem the securities and resell them to new shareholders, but can utilize the open market to do so. As noted earlier, a regional investment banking firm that specializes in banking securities may make a market in your bank/thrift; if so, as the older shareholders exit, the new shareholders may purchase the securities. They will not do so unless you are operating profitably and provide a strong investment return. If you don't have a regional investment banking firm making a market, you should work to do so. Too often, a bank/thrift has a book value of $1,500 or (as I ran across in late 1995) $4,000 per share and wonders why shares are not being bought and sold. Many of the newer shareholders whom you are going to attract will only be able to buy a limited amount of securities. If you have a book value of $4,000 per share, how many people do you imagine are going to be available to buy one round lot? Perhaps you should consider doing the following:

- Value the securities of your bank/thrift or holding company as to their "fair market value."
- Split the stock so as to bring the book value into the range of $25 to $50 per share.
- Split the stock so that the fair market value is between $25 and $50.
- Authorize additional common stock of your financial institution so as to provide a market for new investors.
- Arrange for a regional investment banker to assist you in making a market for your securities.
- Utilize stock dividends rather than cash dividends to replenish and retain capital for purposes of corporate stock redemption.
- Implement a dividend reinvestment plan in order to retain capital and yet place more stock in the market.
- Communicate with your shareholders concerning the liquidity and marketability of their securities so that they know they have the ability to buy and sell in the open market as well as through the corporate stock redemption policy.

PLEASING THE SHAREHOLDERS

There is much more to shareholder relations than simply sending out their dividend checks. I am not discounting the importance of a cash dividend, especially to older shareholders (in terms of years of ownership, not chronological years) who yearly receive cash dividends equal to the basis of their stock. Over the years, many community banks and thrifts have provided cash dividends that are outstanding rates of return on their investment. But there is more than simply the cash or stock dividend. There is the attention paid to the shareholders, not only when they want to sell, but during the year, day by day, week by week. As a part of the campaign to control the shareholder base, and to shift from older to newer shareholders under the control of the board of directors, attention must be paid to the shareholders on a regular basis.

The board of directors should utilize the annual shareholders meeting as a public forum for impressing the shareholders, pressing the flesh, and recognizing the shareholders as the most important segment of the bank or thrift's constituencies. The annual shareholders meeting should be a major social event in the community. By the way, if you are a mutual savings bank or a mutual savings and loan association, simply substitute the word member for shareholder and this subheading applies as much to you as to stock corporation shareholder meetings. Instead of holding the annual meeting at 9 AM or 3 PM in the lobby of the financial institution, it should be held at an appropriate time for your community. There should be a reception and a dinner. Eschew stale cookies and insipid punch! Retire the chairman's wife from the cookie baking detail. Several years ago when I arrived at an annual meeting of a community bank, I found it pulling last year's punch out of the freezer to use at this year's shareholders meeting! You should make the annual shareholders meeting a social event within your community, one that people who are not even shareholders would like to attend. Many of the community banks I have assisted over the years have encouraged townspeople, community leaders, interested bankers from outside their community, and, of course, shareholders and their entire families to attend the annual shareholders meeting. You do not necessarily have to buy dinner for everyone—you could provide meals for the shareholders plus two and others in the group could come at cost. In one small Ohio community, 750 people attended the annual shareholders meeting though the bank had only 125 shareholders! That is a community event! It was interesting to watch women in evening wear (furs and formal gowns) moving across the snow covered walk balancing a cafeteria tray in order to pick up a steak. It was not just a shareholders meeting—it was a happening. Everyone wanted to be there, and the bank benefited. The same can be true for your annual meeting—take advantage of the occasion.

One word of warning—if your president or chairman is unable to talk to a group and absolutely turns the meeting into an agonizing prison sentence, find some way to handle the business portion of the meeting in an entertaining fashion. This meeting should be a highlight of the year, not an ordeal. In addition, while the votes are being tabulated, have an interesting speaker after dinner (or before dinner) who can provide entertainment as well as education on a topic relevant to your community. One year you might engage a speaker who discusses the economics of the country, the next year hire someone to talk on agricultural pricing or economic development within your county. You choose the topic and find an outstanding speaker—don't just bring in a speaker to fill in the void unless you know he will do an outstanding job. Spend the time and extra effort, as well as money, to make your shareholders meeting the best evening of the year.

Before we leave the subject of the annual meeting, where do you think you might find new shareholders? The answer is, at the annual shareholders meeting! Invite those who are not shareholders to come take a look at your bank/thrift at its best. Have them talk to your board of directors and your management and encourage them not only to invest in your institution but to become depositors and borrowers. As your shareholders become older and need to liquidate their investment, look for new investors within the marketplace who can become the backbone for the next 50 years of your financial institution. If you include them in your annual meeting, hustle them just like you would someone for a college fraternity or sorority. You then will have a list of new investors potentially available to assist you in the transition of your shareholder base.

VALUATION OF YOUR SECURITIES

As noted several times in this chapter, it is necessary to value securities of your bank/thrift in order to ascertain the fair market value. Most community banks/thrifts are so illiquid and unmarketable that any trades in securities do not reflect fair market value but are simply random, arbitrary pricing.

If the board of directors determines the price, you could become liable for "fixing the price." It is far better to have the securities valued on a regular basis by an outside, objective, third-party valuation firm that will value the securities on behalf of your institution and provide you with the information necessary to value the securities for corporate stock redemption purposes or other legitimate business purposes. In addition, if you so desire, you can inform your shareholders of what the third-party valuation firm determined the value to be on a regular basis, especially if your securities are not traded actively by a regional investment banker.

The valuation of your securities not only is essential for corporate stock redemption purposes, but also can be utilized concurrently in repurchasing small blocks of stock to establish a floor under the stock price out in the market. In addition, the valuation can be utilized for purposes of ESOP purchase of securities, determining the value of your institution for sale, assessing management's performance as administrators, and providing a public forum when your stock is not traded in the active market. In essence, the valuation of your securities by an outside party takes the monkey off your back as directors and it eliminates your personal or corporate liability if the shareholders do not like the value.

SPLITTING THE STOCK, LOWERING THE BOOK VALUE, AND RAISING THE MARKET PRICE

As noted earlier in Chapter 4, many community banks and thrifts believe that the higher the book value, the better the institution. This is absolute nonsense! If the book value is in excess of $50 a share, then hypothetically the market price is thereabouts or slightly higher, and the stock is about to be priced out of the average shareholder's hands. The book value of $4,000 per share means that a person would need $400,000 in order to buy a round lot (100 shares). If you know of several round lot purchasers in your community, send them over to me—I need to borrow. If you were to split that stock 100 to 1, then the stock would have a book value of $40 a share and you could purchase a round lot for $4,000. The people within your marketplace are much more capable of buying 100 shares at $40 per share than at $4,000 per share. Psychologically, the more shares a shareholder has, the happier he or she is. They would prefer to hold 100 shares at $40 than one share at $4,000—just ask any shareholder. The obvious reason is that at that price they can get rid of 100 shares easier than they can get rid of one share.

If you split the stock, thus decreasing the book value, you increase the demand for the stock, assuming ceteris paribus (i.e., all other things remaining equal). Let me give you an illustration of one of my clients last year. One of the banks in the market had just sold to a statewide bank holding company. It sold for 1.5 times book. My client was selling in the market for $23, only two-thirds of the $35 book value. The stock was valued at $43 to $46 per share on a corporate stock redemption basis, and the bank then decided to buy back 5 percent of it at $45 a share. One would worry that perhaps more than 5 percent of the stock would come rushing into the bank holding company. Actually, only 100 shares more than 5 percent were tendered. Their price is no longer $23 in the market, it is now $45. Another example was the bank holding company formation where the commercial bank had a book value of $1,800 but was selling for only $600. The value of the bank was $2,400 and as a part of the formation, the stock was split 50 to 1, which resulted in a $36 book value at the time of consummation. However, the stock at that point in time was selling at $60 in the market, which was equivalent to $3,000 a share and the simple formation of the bank holding company with the stock split included increasing the price from $12 a share to $60 a share. The shareholders benefited by a 5 to 1 increase in the price of the stock. This is the way to satisfy your shareholders as a community financial institution. A secondary but still significant benefit is that the increase in the market price of the stock inhibits a possible takeover by outside parties.

Please always remember as directors of banks/thrifts that you are responsible to the shareholders. If you keep the price arbitrarily low so that you can buy stock at the expense of the shareholders, it will come back to haunt you. When you decide to split the stock, lower the book value, increase the marketability and liquidity of your stock, and make your community bank a survivor, you as directors will not be able to engage in self-dealing anymore. I am not recommending this—but before you decide to do all the splitting and so on, buy all the stock you want. Once you start to split the stock to make the securities liquid and marketable, you are out of business. A lot more community banks/thrifts would survive if the directors refused to self-deal and thought of the shareholders and the community first.

RECOMMENDATIONS

Value your corporate securities and find out what you are worth for different purposes, such as corporate stock redemption, ESOP valuation, and for-sale value:

- Analyze your shareholders list and determine their age, number of shares, residency, status of estate planning and so on.
- Contact your largest shareholders and institute written agreements to purchase their stock at the time of death or when they need to sell.
- Plan the capital of your bank/thrift holding company and/or commercial bank/thrift so that there is adequate capital to repurchase the securities back from the shareholders if needed.
- Adopt a corporate stock redemption policy to permit the repurchase of stock from your shareholders when financially prudent under the Business Judgment Rule, and make sure you have the financial resources.
- Obtain standby lines of credit from institutional investors to finance borrowings in case of a need to repurchase securities instantaneously.
- Hold outstanding annual shareholder/member meetings and promote the financial institution to your shareholders, customers, and townspeople.
- Maintain a list of new investors and promote your financial institution as a future investment to them.
- Split the stock to improve the market price so as to attract new investors while keeping potential bidders at bay.

CHAPTER 6

Community and Financial Leadership

"The greatest advantage of a community banking financial institution is its contact with the local community." "Multibank holding companies siphon deposits out of local communities." "No bank holding companies or branch systems serve the local community." If you have read or heard sentiments like these, then you have been listening to the independent state and federal trade associations talk about the advantages of being an independent community bank. The fascinating thing is that basically these kinds of statements are true. However, they are not an intrinsic attribute of a community banking financial institution. They are a result of community banks and thrifts operating in the local markets and, over the past 50 years, developing financial leadership tendencies within the communities, vis-à-vis the bank holding company affiliate, multistate branching system, or the thrift holding company affiliate. Community banks do not have an innate advantage over multibank affiliates or branching systems. You, as readers, whether you are directors or officers, know of high-quality, competent individuals working for the opposition. Bank and thrift officers, staff members, and directors who represent multibank holding company affiliates, statewide branching systems, and thrift organizations are no different than any of your directors and officers. They go to church, they take part in school activities, they are involved in community leadership positions, they provide administrative leadership throughout the banking market. Why then are you better, and how can we make sure over the next few years that you remain better as community and financial leaders, vis-à-vis the multistate holding company affiliates, the multistate interstate branching operations, and the multinational banking operations that will compete either within or on the periphery of your banking market?

How then do community banking organizations, whether they be banks or thrifts, dominate community and financial leadership within the banking markets? The answer is continuity. The one liability imposed upon the banking markets and your local community by the multibank holding companies, thrift holding companies, and branching systems is the lack of continuity of their outstanding officers. As a part of a corporate system, there is a philosophical desire to eventually end up in Mecca, or Cleveland, whichever is closer. Thus, the branch managers desire larger branches, larger cities, and eventually the head office town, while bank holding company affiliate presidents and senior officers desire promotions to larger affiliates, perhaps even a corporate headquarters job. There are those who represent the money center banks and bank holding companies as well as the interstate thrift operations that would like to stay in your community and compete with you over the next 10 to 12 years, and even if they don't desire promotion to a larger banking operation, the corporate system demands such change. Thus, the turnover of your competitors is the major reason why the community banking operation survives the leadership advantage within the community over the long run. The locally oriented community banking financial institution is the top of the corporate structure. The officers and directors are in Mecca when they are within your community, and there is no need or desire to go elsewhere. Unless you drive away your outstanding corporate bankers, they will be there to serve the community and provide the community and financial leadership necessary for your community to survive. However, this innate advantage has to be exploited, and the purpose of this chapter is to outline ways by which your financial institution can do a better job in order to serve your community and to provide the economic and financial foundation for its survival.

GOALS OF THE DIRECTORS

Directors supervise and monitor the activities of the financial institution. They are, of course, individuals who reside within or near the communities served by the community banking financial institution, and one of the reasons they have been elected to the board is because of their solid community activities, local reputation, credibility, and veracity as well as their participation in various facets of your community. They become the foundation of the community leadership of your market area. It is most appropriate to ask for the resignation of, or simply not renominate, directors of your community banks and thrifts who no longer reside in the market, vacation for extended periods of time (three to four months) in sunny climes, or have retired from their vocation and no longer participate in the community activities. You will note that I have not mentioned the word *age* anywhere in this paragraph. I believe that bank and thrift directors can serve the community regardless of age. There are people just as senile and demented at 40 as others are at 70, except we call them "eccentric." However, when an individual director has retired from his or her vocation, profession, or job, and no longer is involved in community activities, then that individual should step aside and permit new blood onto the banking board. I have been a bank consultant for over 30 years and believe that those bank and thrift boards who are aged and retired also have become retarded as to aggressiveness, attentiveness to current regulations, and change. You may want to create maturity on your board by having older directors, but you should not end up with a fossilized board by simply having old people who have been together for a long time. As a part of your annual assessment of your directors, you should determine how active they still are in the community as well as how much time per year they spend within the community. If they fail these tests, they should be retired.

Your board of directors *must* be an active, committed group of individuals who are omnipresent within your banking market. They must be active in your local, religious, civic, educational, and social organizations. They have to be your eyes and ears to the ground, and they are the ones representing your community bank or thrift as a "flag" to the community. If your directors are not, they should be replaced. If they are, you have an innate advantage over other nonmarket headquartered financial institutions. The ability to be seen and to be known as a community bank director is almost as important as what the individual might do or say in terms of a community bank or thrift's survivability. I am not suggesting that the board of directors go door to door hustling business for the bank or thrift. I am not suggesting that the board of directors carry marketing brochures and business cards daily and hand them out Japanese-style. I am suggesting that the board of directors be visible within the banking market (the communities served by the financial institution). The directors are the link between the customers and residents of the banking market and the bank/thrift. If they are in Florida, Texas, or Arizona, or if they are retired at home raising roses or playing golf, then they cannot be the communications and coordination link between the people they represent and the bank/thrift.

SENIOR MANAGEMENT

Let's face it—a significant portion of the president/CEO's job is to be a representative of the bank/thrift to the banking market. She should spend approximately 50 percent of her time on community activities, economic development, and financial leadership. The president/CEO should not be stuck behind her desk, making routine loans, and managing the personnel of the bank/thrift on a day-to-day basis. After World War II, Army won its football games by having Mr. Outside and Mr. Inside. Your bank/thrift needs a Mr. or Ms. Inside and Mr. and Ms. Outside. Your president should be Mr. or Ms. Outside, while the executive vice president or senior vice president, whoever is second in charge, should be Mr. or Ms. Inside. Thus, your president should be a people person, a community leader, one who is pushing for economic development and change within your banking market, and one who is dedicated to civic activities as an integral part of her job.

Since it is important for your president/CEO to be your community representative, it is also imperative upon you as directors to make sure that the banking operations run smoothly. This may mean that you have to have an extra officer somewhere in the hierarchy so that the president can spend his time out within the community representing your financial institution. This is not a high price to pay if you wish to survive as a community banking institution over the next 10 to 20 years. Contact between the bank/thrift and the community is essential for your survival and that can only be done through direct participation and leadership positions within the banking market. You must provide financial resources within the bank/thrift and make sure that your president/CEO has enough time to be an integral part of the community. In fact, you should grade him on how well he does and how much time he spends on behalf of your financial institution.

A final comment: If your president/CEO is not capable of providing the outside contacts and leadership, it may be time to change things within your financial institution in order to be able to cement the financial institution community relationship.

What about the other senior management? Obviously, if you have one individual spending approximately 50 percent of his time out within the community, the others can't spend that amount of time. There is no reason for them not to be involved. A portion of their merit evaluation each year should be based on their community involvement. Bankers—especially customer service people and lending officers—are generally gregarious, extroverted people. They should be expected to be involved in their communities, whether it be educational, religious, social, or cultural activities. They come from disparate backgrounds, are involved in different religious denominations, and have differing social and recreational interests. However, wherever they are involved, they represent your banking institution, and in so doing, tie together your financial institution with the community's development and strength. You should determine a percentage of the evaluation, such as 25 to 33 percent of the merit increase based upon the quantity and quality of community activities of your senior management. These are the individuals who will proceed up the career ladder and eventually become the top officers of the banking institution. In so doing they will be a symbol of your institution. They should be well known, well respected, and involved extensively within your community.

STAFF

Staff includes your middle and lower management as well as your clerical, hourly employees. Do not ignore them as individuals who can assist in the financial leadership of your community. These individuals should be encouraged to participate in the community, choosing whatever types of activities fit their personal needs and interests. You should encourage them to be involved in at least three different community activities. Then make sure that they are held accountable for having done so and that you reward them if they do so participate. Finally, you should be cognizant of the time and effort necessary to fulfill their obligations. You will not achieve strong community and financial leadership without also allowing your staff the time to do the job. Not only should they be encouraged to become involved intimately within the community, they must also be given time to do the best job possible.

SYSTEM FOR COMMUNITY INVOLVEMENT

The best way to involve your management and staff in the community is to set up a matrix of involvement. For example, senior and middle management should be involved in at least five community activities. Your staff should be involved in at least three. You do not choose which they are, except for a few foundation activities that you are involved in traditionally—for example, the United Way, the Chamber of Commerce, civic service clubs, and local economic development agencies. You should prepare a list of all of the community activities available for your management and staff to be involved in. They should select on their own, especially since people may be more or less religious, more or less athletically inclined, more or less recreationally inclined, more or less financially inclined, and so on. Activities should all be weighted equally, and you should evaluate staff's participation yearly as a part of their merit evaluations. You should encourage additional or supplemental activities, and you should be lenient in approving activities suggested by your management and staff. Your staff should know that if they do not become involved in community activities, it will adversely impact their career success and could, in the ultimate, cause them to lose their employment. If you plan to survive as an independent community banking organization, your ties to the local community must be so strong as to be almost a Siamese twin, and you can't do so with only a half-hearted community involvement by your people. They must understand the importance of the extensive and intensive involvement of the staff in the activities of the community.

ECONOMIC DEVELOPMENT

Your bank or thrift cannot finance every economic development project that pops up within your market area. However, you should be intricately involved with any economic development project that surfaces. The worst possible thing you can do as a bank/thrift is to oppose private or government economic and financial development within the communities served by your bank/thrift. Local community banks or thrifts are expected to promote and to lend the expertise necessary to develop the communities economically and financially. As noted earlier, you are not necessarily expected to finance every project, but in conjunction with local, state, and federal government bodies you are expected to help promote and attain corporate financing for the economic developments. If the projects are private and proprietary, you should be involved in obtaining such funds through correspondent banks, institutional investors, banker's banks, and private individual sources. Since you are the financial leader within the community, you are expected to provide the expertise to promote the continuation of your banking market communities through such economic development. Not to do so may become a death knell for your institution. Let me give you an example:

Almost a decade ago in a local community in Michigan whose name is not relevant, the president of the locally owned independent community bank opposed the extension of sewer facilities and a hospital expansion within the community. He felt the community could not afford it. His actions tarred the entire community bank, its directors, its employees, and especially its activities as negative and pessimistic, with a status quo brush. Over the next year the bank lost almost 10 percent of its deposits and fell out of favor within the marketplace. A new bank was chartered to oppose a negative reputation of the local community bank. Finally, the local community bank was sold and became an affiliate of a statewide banking organization, after the local president had been unceremoniously retired. Here is a classic case of corporate hari-kari, all because the bank president, on his own, decided to determine the future course of economic development within the community. His unilateral, arbitrary decision ruined the future of the bank.

Economic and financial development is a win–win situation within your market. If you oppose it, it is like being opposed to God, mother, and country. There is no way that your financial intermediary cannot win through increased economic development. Even if the economic development does nothing other than maintain local employment, that's better than losing the local employment base and having less economic potential. On the other hand, if economic development fosters new employment, extends sewer lines, builds sewer plants, and develops shopping centers, how can you possibly lose? You may not have to agree with every type of economic development or every individual project, but your people, from the directors down to the staff, should be involved in developing a consensus for such development. You should be a part of the solution and not the cause of the problem. If your community does not continue to develop economically and financially, then your banking market over time will stagnate and start to decline, and even the most efficiently run community bank or thrift cannot survive in the long term in such an environment. Thus, economic development and involvement by your directors, senior management, and staff are essential for the long-term survivability of your institution as well as your communities.

PROMOTING ECONOMIC DEVELOPMENT

Each banking market is different. Thus, the comments within this subsection may or may not be relevant to your local market. Your board of directors and staff should promote economic and financial development within your market. As noted above, it is essential to your survival. How you do it is what is different from market to market. In some markets there is a well-developed, competent, professional economic development team, known alternatively as a development authority, chamber of commerce, community improvement corporation, or some other similar name. If such is available within your marketplace, don't duplicate the process. You should assist the organized development group through direct financing from your own coffers as well as the personal involvement of your directors, management, and staff. On the other hand, if such is not available within the marketplace, you have two alternatives. First, you can help develop such a local economic development group by working with your competitor financial institutions, local and state governments, and so on. Second, you can promote economic and financial development within your own banking market directly through utilizing your own staff to promote factory entry, shopping center development, residential housing development, wholesale or retail trade development, and so on. This means that you will have to have one or more individuals whose job responsibilities aren't economic development solely, but in your community, that may bring the best result if an organized professional group is not in place and productive. Either way, you should be involved directly and extensively in the promotion of your community and marketplace, and in doing so, your financial rewards will be through improved business activity of your financial institution and all financial institutions in general.

RECOMMENDATIONS

- Directors must be extensively involved in community activities through yearly participation and personal involvement.
- Approximately 50 percent of your president/CEO's time should be in community activities, economic and financial development, and personal involvement outside the financial institution.
- Senior management must be extensively involved in the community in at least five community activities throughout the year.
- Lower management and staff must be involved in the community as a part of the financial leadership demanded of financial institutions for at least three activities.

- Your financial institution must become or continue to be a financial leader within the banking market and personal involvement in the activities necessary to develop and/or at least maintain the economic viability of your market.
- Finance or promote economic activity—it's a win–win situation.
- Avoid self-destructive activity by opposing economic and financial development within your banking market.

CHAPTER 7

Survival through Internal and External Growth

If You Do Not Grow, You Die!

Here is a homework assignment for you. Pick up your Uniform Bank Performance Report (UBPR) or your Uniform Thrift Performance Report (UTPR) and turn to the financial ratio comparing your cost estimates to that of your peer group. I'm not really interested in the peer group; I'm really interested in your cost of funds. In order to remain precisely the same relative size that you were last year, you must grow by at least your cost of funds this year. I am assuming that there are no net withdrawals from interest that you have accrued to your customers' accounts. If you look at your recent depository growth and find that you have not kept pace with your cost of funds, you are falling behind. You are not growing, you're dying. Now take a look at the peer group cost of funds ratio. Are you above or below them—are they forced to grow faster than you or not as fast? Also look at the rate of deposit growth of your peer group. Is it faster than your growth? If so, you are not growing as fast as your competitors. Now, realistically, the peer group information is not necessarily within your own banking market. So compute the rate of growth on a compound annual growth basis, of the bank and thrift competitors within your banking market, including not only community banks and thrifts that you believe that you most compete with, but also those giant multistate, multinational pariahs you are always concerned about. What is the growth rate in deposits within your marketplace? Are you in an environment that is static, secularly declining, or growing twice as fast as the state average? Your community bank/thrift is not alone in the universe. You compete with other financial institutions, and your growth rate is critical, vis-à-vis other financial institutions.

WHY GROWTH IS IMPORTANT

Over the past decade and a half, bankers have been besieged with demands for profitability and capital adequacy. Whereas growth was important in the 1970s, it went out of favor in the 1980s. There was no reason to become the fastest growing failed bank in your county. Most financial institutions that grew the fastest during the 1980s failed miserably—they were called savings and loans and they attempted to turn operational deficits into profits through growth, and it didn't work. Growth is second to profitability and capital adequacy, but growth is essential for profitability. Profitability is the foundation for capital adequacy over time. Growth is important because it permits increased resources within the financial institution over time. As an illustration, if your bank/thrift remains the same deposit size, the only increase in revenue that will arise will be from increased market rates or changing composition in your loan portfolio. Increase in costs of funds will derive from either increased market rates or changing composition of deposit categories. Assuming the same increase in asset rates as in depository rates, then your net interest margin is the same, and there is no net benefit. Thus, over time, if you remain relatively constant in size, your noninterest expenses will increase more than your noninterest income and you will be less profitable. You need increased size in terms of assets and deposits in order to increase the revenue base of your organization so as to permit (1) expense increases either through salary increases or other noninterest expenses and (2), even more importantly, additions to your staff that increase the expertise and depth of management. A stagnant financial intermediary cannot improve its management quality and expertise; a stagnant financial intermediary becomes impotent and, even more importantly, unnecessary.

GROWING ON A COMPOUND ANNUAL GROWTH RATE (CAGR) BASIS

Let's just make an assumption that you haven't grown in the past five years. Your profitability has been in excess of 1 percent rate of return on average assets and you have a 9 percent capital base. You are doing just fine from a safety and solvency standpoint. However, you haven't grown. Let's find out why!

The first thing to do is to examine how the other competitors are doing within your banking market or markets. However you compete, how are you doing in relation to them? First of all, you don't necessarily have to change current behavior. I'm asking you to analyze the situation and determine whether you are following the proper course, or whether the others are and you just haven't become flexible enough to change. If, for example, using our assumptions, the remainder of the market is growing by 8 percent on a CAGR basis in deposits per annum, you are flat dead in the water, obviously not competitive. In real terms, you are not only constant in size, but falling behind in percentage of market share. You are becoming less relevant annually. On the other hand, if you are remaining constant in size, and the rest of the market has a negative growth in deposits, the opposite is true. This is why just looking at your own financial statements may not be appropriate analysis. You must compare yourself with your competitors within the market so that you can determine how the whole group is doing, including yourselves.

If the market is growing and you're not, you are going to have to determine how to grow to keep competitive. If your banking market is not growing (i.e., is stagnant or declining), then to continue to grow as a financial intermediary, you are going to have to find another market. This means external growth through either branching or merger beyond your current market area. Either way, controlled, sustainable, practical growth is crucial to your survivability as a community bank/thrift, and if it is not available within your own market, you are going to have to find it elsewhere.

STRANGLING, TRADITIONAL THOUGHTS

Bank and thrift interest rates are based on tradition. They are also based on what the current rates are at your institution. If you desire to grow by internal means, you must strangle tradition and develop interest rates that will be competitive in the marketplace. As an illustration, think carefully about how you prepared and/or approved last year's financial budget for your bank/thrift. Did you not take the previous year's expenses and then increase them by a percentage? Or, did you go back to zero and ascertain the expenses as if you had not even operated the previous year? I really don't need to have your answer—you obviously just increased the previous year's expenses by a percentage. That's the traditional way. It has no bearing as to what your expenses should be, but simply relates this year's expenses to last year's expenses as if last year's expenses were appropriate. Perhaps your marketing budget should have been four times as large this year as it is, maybe your payroll should have been 80 percent of what it is, or maybe you should have spent more on branch expansion, and so on. If you simply develop a budget year after year based upon last year's budget, you are thinking traditionally and not looking at opportunities within the marketplace. The same is true if you price your deposits and your loans based upon what they have been rather than what would be competitive within your marketplace, so that you could grow by a certain percentage and yet remain independently profitable, safe, and solvent.

Before you can determine what the interest rates are, you must determine how fast you wish to grow. This has to be done by computer modeling, assuming what price differential is needed between your interest rates on competitive products, vis-à-vis your competitors. You can grow faster than your competitors if you price your deposits higher. You can also remember the old adage "Advertise when you're hot, disappear when you're not" and thus advertise your higher rates and, as you lower them to be in the middle of the competitive range, continue your advertising. Increasing your internal growth in deposits and assets depends upon concerted effort on behalf of your asset and liability committee (ALCO) as well as your senior management in determining exactly how fast you want to grow, what interest rates you want to pay, and what impact, if any, the increased cost of funds will have on your net interest margin and, thus, profitability. If you don't have the capital to start branches de novo or acquire other banks or thrifts, then you may have to grow through internal generation of deposits. This is a decision you have to make in order to survive.

INTERNAL GROWTH THROUGH BRANCHING

Branching your bank or thrift is a form of internal growth if you branch de novo. If you purchase another bank or thrift's branch(es), then it is a form of external growth, which will be discussed below. Tradition must be stifled, stabbed, and buried. As a banking consultant for over 30 years, I still run across community banks and thrifts that have never branched even though they may be 50 to 125 years old. Not only have they not branched, they haven't even thought about it or, if they have thought about it, they have never made a decision to do so. Branching is a horizontal extension of your current products and services, and promotes your survivability through increased deposit growth and market share. Branching is nothing more than another teller's window, separated from the main office by distance. If you can operate a commercial bank or savings and loan, you can operate a branching system as well. You have to determine whether there is a community, township, or market area in which you can operate and make money. You should never branch simply to branch, but it should be an economic/financial decision based upon market analysis with profitability being the foundation for your decision. There may be a community where there has never been a branch, or a community where some other financial institution has closed an office, or an area where there is already competition and you decide to branch de novo. Branching becomes a critical method of internal growth of your financial institution—a method as important as interest rate adjustments, maybe even more important, in terms of expanding your market area for your own products and services.

EXTERNAL GROWTH

The first type of external growth is to purchase other financial institutions' branches. While you are doing your analysis of where you might place your branches on a de novo basis, you will be analyzing economic and demographic statistics on communities within the marketplace. You should examine all other depository financial institutions' offices. If you like a certain community or a particular part of a city, why not find out if that other institution wants to sell its office? In the past five years money center regional-oriented bank holding companies and thrifts have been selling individual branches or clumps of branches. Today, one of your best chances for external growth is to purchase somebody else's branch and make it a part of your institution. Ten years ago if you had called up another banker or thrift manager and asked if you could buy one of her branches, she would have yelled at you and hung up. Today, managers consider the offer seriously, and perhaps they will allow you to make an offer. Furthermore, these multibank holding companies and thrifts are selling branches as a part of a new corporate strategy. Keep apprised of opportunities within your market area. Realistically, there is nothing different from buying a branch than from buying an entire financial institution, except that it's cheaper. If you are going to have to pay a premium on the deposits you purchase, then you may get stuck with the other financial institution's people, which may not be so bad. It does permit you to grow. One of my clients recently was able to purchase a $20 million branch from a multistate bank holding company. It's only a $20 million branch, but if you consider the fact that my client only has a $40 million bank, it becomes a big deal. Depository growth in this rural, agriculturally oriented market has been zippo, nil, flat, zero, and terrible. External growth through purchasing somebody else's branch that they don't like is outstanding for my client. The client now has $60 million of assets and resources, rather than $40 million, and although this will not make him one of the top 10 banking organizations in the United States, it provides additional resources to survive as a community bank. You should consider aggressively purchasing other financial institutions' branches as an alternative to branching on your own.

Merger and acquisition are also forms of external growth. I am assuming, of course, that you are doing the buying and not selling. In order to remain a community bank/thrift, you have to purchase somebody else without losing control of the consolidated operation. Mergers occur when you purchase another institution and combine them with yours; acquisitions occur when you acquire another institution and make it an autonomous subsidiary of your holding company. For our purposes, mergers and acquisitions are interchangeable because they add to our growth potential as a financial intermediary regardless of whether (1) we are in consolidated merged form or (2) we have more than one banking subsidiary. You may decide to merge the banking operations if the bank or thrift you purchase is within your current banking market, and you may decide to acquire the financial institution as a subsidiary if it is in another banking market and it makes good financial business sense to keep it as a separate affiliate with its own name, staff, and so on. Regardless of whether it is a branch or an affiliate, external growth through merger and acquisition becomes an important alternative for your survival and markets where internal growth has not been sufficient and/or opportunities for de novo branching are limited. Furthermore, you may pick up excellent, competent, professional managers from the merger/acquisition, and the availability of such bank/thrifts may be a result of director and management interest in increasing shareholders liquidity rather than operating in the future. Thus, mergers and acquisitions become an excellent source of external growth and should be considered as important to your survival as any other form of growth methodology.

RECOMMENDATIONS

- Survival demands growth.
- If you do not grow, you will not survive.
- Create internal growth through market interest rate adjustments.
- Branching de novo promotes growth of your community bank/thrift.
- Encourage alternative growth through purchase of bank and savings and loan branches.
- Create external growth through merger and acquisition of other community bank/thrifts.
- Develop a corporate marketing philosophy to undertake internal and external growth as a means of corporate survival through appropriate controlled growth in assets and deposits.

CHAPTER 8

Cultural Change in Community Banking Survival

It should be obvious by now that the major theme of this book is breaking the mold of tradition in order to survive as a community banking financial institution. It does not make much difference how large your organization is, where you are located, whether you are a bank or a thrift, or whether you are nationally or state-chartered. What you need to do in order to survive in this increasingly competitive marketplace bears no resemblance to what you have done in the past 50 to 100 years. Regardless of how successful your institution has been, there is no assurance that your success will continue tomorrow. Your institution may be granted legal perpetuity in your state, but you cannot be granted even one day of economic or financial perpetuity. beyond the day you become bankrupt. You must continue to operate profitably and within the constraints of regulation. You must operate in a safe and solvent manner, and in doing so you must provide the services necessary to meet the needs of the public. The purpose of this chapter is to try to convince you that corporate cultural change may be necessary in order for you to survive.

THE TRANSACTION CULTURE

It is important to remind you that scholars, fellow bankers, regulators, and various banking publications have been informing you as directors and senior managers for the past decade that the industry has changed and that you cannot expect the customers to come to you anymore. As an author, I have repeatedly commented concerning the need for a sales/marketing culture. My presentations reiterate and reverberate with recommendations and requirements to directors and senior managers to wake up and start selling! I wish I could report that all of this emphasis has been of value—whether it came from me or is the work of many others. Unfortunately, every time I consult at a community bank/thrift, I discover the same traditional mode of operations that I found a decade ago. The message has not sunk in! There is a real need to change, and if you do not change, you will not survive.

The traditional methodology used to be to sit at the bank and wait for the customers to come in the door. Once they came through the door, you processed their transactions and they left. Whether it is inside the bank, at the drive-in window, or even at an ATM, the transaction cultural model was founded on providing quality service for whatever the customers wanted, when they wanted it, and at *your* locations. In years to come, this will be a surefire formula for slow death at your financial institution.

SALES/MARKETING CULTURE

This is a markedly different approach to banking. In the sales culture model, as a bank or thrift, you go out and find your customers, deliver services at their locations, compete aggressively against your competitors, and do not take no for an answer. You become an insurance salesperson, a brokerage representative, or a real estate salesperson. You do not sit in your office with your feet on your desk and wait for customers to arrive. Over 50 percent of your time will be spent out of your office calling on customers. More importantly, you will spend time calling on potential customers and trying to get their business away from another financial institution.

The most surprising aspect of changing from a transaction culture to a sales culture is that it really does not take much money and effort to do so. You do not need to build any new buildings. You do not need to hire any new personnel (although you may have to retrain your existing people). You really do not need any additional equipment, except perhaps a company car so your lenders can travel around the community, and a few cellular phones so they can keep in close contact. A sales culture is not a matter of brick and mortar, personnel, or equipment—it is a matter of strategy, perception, and the ability to compete in the new competitive arena.

WHAT YOU NEED TO DO

You will need to convert your personnel from order takers to salespeople. Bankers have traditionally despised the word *sales*. It has always reminded them of someone selling used cars, appliances, and insurance. Sales is an honorable profession. (I have to say that. My own father was sales manager for Perfect Circle Corporation, a piston ring manufacturer. I grew up believing that sales was so important that Perfect Circle could not survive without a strong sales department.) As a banking consultant for the past 30 years, every time I hear the word *sales*, I hear derision and scoffing by bankers and thrift personnel. Selling banking products and services to the public wherever they are located, making sure their institution's services are available 24 hours a day, and constantly being on duty is a new approach for bankers to take, but it is not unusual from how other professions conduct business. There is nothing for bankers to be ashamed of if they are called salespeople. The more you sell, the better the financial performance of your institution and the more secure your employment.

THE IMPORTANCE OF DIRECTORS IN ESTABLISHING A SALES/MARKETING CULTURE

As directors, you are not expected to run around town selling the products and services of your community banking institution. You are not expected to carry brochures and business cards. However, you are expected to provide resources and provide the backbone for establishing and maintaining a sales culture at your community bank/thrift. Here is what directors should do:

- Approve policies that mandate the sales and marketing culture for your institution.
- Inform management that sales and business development calls are an integral part of merit evaluations.
- Provide the necessary resources for management's implementation of the sales culture within the institution.
- Monitor officer and staff call programs.
- Train management and staff to sell products and services through in-house training, seminars, and conferences.
- Utilize incentive compensation (commissions, bonuses, etc.) to reward outstanding sales.

- Inform management and staff that employees paid commissions and bonuses will earn what they deserve, not just a traditional, historical salary.

As I look around board rooms during my strategic planning engagements, I have found retailers and manufacturers as members of the board. These are the most sales-conscious and sales-oriented board members. If your board is composed primarily of lawyers, accountants, housewives, farmers, university professors, and bankers, no wonder you cannot understand the importance of marketing and sales. You need professions and vocations that must make their living by selling themselves and their products. Sales and revenue come to you; you do not have to go out and sell. This is because laws and regulations force them to use your services and you have more business than you can solicit—you sit in your offices and the economy forces your clients to come to you. Listen to your board members who make their living by selling their products and services competitively in the open market. They know what it is like to sell—and to sell successfully.

If the board of directors does not push sales and marketing, then the financial institution will be unable to shift from the transaction order taking model to the sales/marketing culture. The board of directors through its mandates and its rewards can force a recalcitrant management and staff to change. This change may not take place overnight—it may take years to accomplish, but the institution will reap the rewards.

THE ROLE OF THE DIRECTORS

Finally, the board of directors should hold the president/CEO of the institution accountable for the transformation from transaction order taking to the sales culture. If the resources are given to the president, then he or she is responsible for the implementation of the programs and the results therefrom. The board of directors is not expected to monitor the sales/marketing program on a daily basis, but must act in a monitoring/supervision capacity no differently than their other responsibilities. However, if officers are not performing their outside business solicitations, if employees are not cross-selling, and if business has not increased and revenue has not been enhanced, then the president/CEO should be held responsible. The sales and marketing culture will not become dominant in your financial institution through prayer or magic wand waving. A sales and marketing culture takes time, resources, effort, and, most importantly, the threat of a cattle prod. After one decade of the sales and marketing culture being introduced to banking, it has not yet become endemic to the banking industry. This means there is a lot of work to do to make sure that your management and staff converts to a sales/marketing culture.

WHAT MANAGEMENT MUST DO

If we assume that the board of directors is Congress, then the bank/thrift president becomes the administration implementing the act of Congress. The president, as a member of the board of directors, promotes policy. As president/CEO, he or she implements the policies as set forth by the board. The president has the day-to-day responsibility of transforming the bank/thrift from the traditional transaction-oriented financial intermediary into the new sales/marketing dynamo. As noted earlier, failure to meet that responsibility should result in dismissal of the president. There are too many other financial intermediaries out there that are effectively selling, and waiting for the customer to arrive at your door may be a fatal mistake.

What should the president do? He should delegate the sales/marketing model to his vice president of marketing (if one exists), and then monitor the establishment and implementation of such a program. If the community bank/thrift is large enough, the president should rely on the institution's professional staff to develop the program and implement the procedures, and then assist in the analysis of the results and reward the winners and discipline those that don't get with the program. Merit evaluations should be based upon the quality of business development, officer solicitation, and cross-selling, all of which have been specifically weighted as to their merit and all of which have been emphasized to the staff as to their importance.

The most important thing that the president can do is fire someone. This may sound crass, but if you are attempting to change the cultural atmosphere and environment of your community bank/thrift, and you have reluctant transformees, then eliminating someone after an appropriate, rational merit evaluation might be akin to getting a mule's attention with a 2x4 to the head! Your staff may not believe that you really want an officer call program, business solicitation results on a daily basis, cross-selling to customers in the bank offices, telephone calls made to potential customers, visits made to existing customers, and so on. If there is an outstanding example of lousy salesmanship, poor managerial attitude, and general slothful performance, then elimination of that individual as a management or staff member may be the most effective method of attaining a sales and marketing transformation. Remember, the president/CEO was not hired to run a charity. Your financial institution is a for-profit business—and the only way to make profits is to create revenue and lower expenses.

RECOMMENDATIONS

- Develop corporate policies to promote a sales and marketing culture.
- Provide the corporate resources necessary to implement a sales/marketing culture.
- Delegate responsibility for implementation of a sales/marketing culture to the president/CEO.
- Reinforce the president's delegative authority to implement a sales/marketing culture.
- Hold the president/CEO accountable for sales/marketing and its various programs of implementation.
- The president should hold staff and senior and junior officers responsible for implementation of sales/marketing programs.
- Failure to perform the duties assigned to transform the institution into a sales/marketing-oriented community financial organization should result in unemployment.

The Significance of Profitability, Capital Adequacy, and Asset/ Liability Management to the Survivability of Community Banking Institutions

Community banks and thrifts are for-profit corporations and associations. Even mutual savings and loans and mutual savings banks have to make a profit or they do not survive. Community banks and thrifts are not charitable organizations; they are businesses. The most important thing you do as the board of directors and senior management of your financial institution is to make a profit. Profitability is the foundation for capital adequacy and safe, solvent banking. If you are not profitable, then you become less capitally adequate, and as your asset quality diminishes, you become less and less a viable financial intermediary. The purpose of this chapter is to stress the importance of being the most profitable financial intermediary you can and, as such, emphasize at board meetings and at management sessions the importance of profitability, capital adequacy, and asset and liability management.

FINANCIAL STATEMENTS AND THEIR IMPORTANCE

Bank and thrift boards I have known and loved over the past 30 years of financial consulting really hate analyzing financial statements. For verification of my opinion, look around your board and simultaneously do a self-analysis of yourself: You really do not like analyzing financial statements because you don't understand them! For 20 years I have presented directors' seminars and when I get to the two sessions entitled "understanding financial statements" and "ratio analysis in your institution," the majority of the audience cancels out. Why is this so? The answer is simple: The bank and thrift directors with whom I discuss financial statements, accounting statements, and ratio analysis as well as asset and liability management are often individuals who are *not* accounting- and finance-oriented. If they were, they might be bankers. When you look around your board, you will find farmers, lawyers, retailers, manufacturers, union officials, housewives, old sailors, doctors, dentists, veterinarians, ad nauseam, but you very seldom find CPAs. Once in awhile you might find a finance professor from a nearby university. Almost all of your directors are financially illiterate, and they want to remain that way. Most of you have avoided anything more difficult than balancing your bank checking account statement each month. This is not meant to be a personal slam—it is simply a matter of truth. If you were all finance- and accounting-oriented, then you would have been accountants and bankers. I have run across very few clergymen who could balance a checkbook or understand the church budget, and when I have, I have usually run in the opposite direction because they are sharper than most people. Doctors, dentists, veterinarians, and other medical professionals are well known for their lack of financial acumen and investment expertise. I realize that these are all generalizations, but realistically, most boards of directors are not bankers and are not accounting- or finance-oriented. Thus, you react uncertainly and hesitantly any time financial statements are analyzed. It is almost impossible for you to act as a check and balance to the management and staff if you don't understand what you are supposed to be auditing and checking. Management can dominate a director–management relationship if you are not strong enough as a board to understand the realities of the financial condition and performance of your institution. The board of directors must be bright enough to be able to know when financial conditions and performance are below par and that the management is "misrepresenting" the quality of the current operations of the institution to the board of directors.

First, you must be trained. The CFO or cashier of your bank/thrift is a good source. If this individual cannot teach you additional accounting and financial skills, then replace her with someone who can. Moreover, most of you utilize an outside CPA firm to assist in preparing taxes or certifying your audit. These individuals can come in and assist you in understanding the financial statements and asset and liability management. In fact, they can provide you with written materials that you can review prior to the discussions. You just have to forget to be nervous and hesitant concerning the fact that you don't understand the area. You should ask questions—the dumber the better—and provide yourself with increased knowledge. Furthermore, as you hire new directors to join your bank or thrift, find individuals who have accounting and financial skills who will buttress you by their expertise and experience.

THE CAMEL AND MACRO SYSTEMS

Why are we discussing profitability, capital adequacy, and asset and liability management? The CAMEL and MACRO systems are really the answer. As directors and senior managers of your bank/thrift, profitability, capital adequacy, asset quality, and the techniques by which to obtain them are essential for your survival. The CAMEL system, as you know, stands for capital (C), asset quality (A), management (M), earnings (E), and liquidity (L). At the same time, the MACRO system for thrifts stands for management (M), asset quality (A), capital (C), rates of return (R), and operation quality (O). These are almost identical measures of the bank/thrift strength and performance. Profitability is measured by the E of CAMEL and the R of MACRO. Earnings drive the financial institution, and community banks and thrifts that are highly profitable seldom have long-term financial problems. Earnings after tax become retained earnings and cash common dividends, and assist in providing above–peer-group capital levels as noted in Chapter 8. High-performance profitability permits for some asset quality mistakes when loans become charge-offs and/or past dues, and high-performance profitability becomes the foundation for increasing the capital base. Since most community banks and thrifts do not declare significant dividends, capital levels increase through retention of earnings after tax. Thus, adequate capital levels can become adequate or even above-adequate levels by simple retention of earnings year after year. The early 1990s are typical examples of cyclical earnings in banking that have made many sick banks and thrifts well.

There is no reason why your financial institution cannot do at least as well as the peer group average. If your management tells you there are reasons why they cannot meet peer group averages, listen to them for one year and fire them the second. It is difficult to believe that you as mature, intellectual, well-reasoned directors are willing to settle for average performance, (i.e., 50 percent of the banks or thrifts in your peer group do better than you while 50 percent do worse). Why not attempt to achieve financial performance 50 percent higher than the averages or some other level that you are willing to accept. Why should you accept mediocrity? If you accept mediocrity, then you will have a mediocre, average staff, mediocre, average lending officers, mediocre, average presidents and senior managers, mediocre, average financial results, mediocre financial condition of your financial institution, and guess what—a mediocre board. The standard for years has always been 1 percent rate of return on average assets. You should be able to do 1 percent in your sleep in the environment of banking today. In fact, your peer group may be averaging a 1.25 percent rate of return on average assets. You should be above the average peer group. Don't go looking for another peer group whose performance is lower just so that you can look relatively good—compare yourself to the appropriate peer group and attempt to achieve more.

CAPITAL ADEQUACY

Over the past two decades, the banking regulators have changed the standards of capital more than they have changed any other accounting and/or financial standards. Every year or two the FFIEC, the Federal Reserve System, the OTS, the OCC, the FDIC, and the FHLB all attempt to change the capital standards impacting international banks, multinational banks, moneycenter banks, and community banks and thrifts. If you as members of the board of directors are confused as financial standards change, join the club! Over the past 20 years I have written two books on capital planning, and the most favorable comment I can make about my own books is that they were out of date by the time they were published because every time I turned around, the capital standards were changed again. I am not going to burden you as a reader by attempting to explain what the capital standards are at the time of the writing of this book. That would be nonsensical and would probably prompt you to either throw this book as far as possible or salute the porcelain goddess. I am, however, going to discuss the importance of capital adequacy and your acknowledgment of same as a member of the board of directors or senior management.

I have a pet theory that has never been discredited. My pet theory is that if you have too much capital (i.e., 50 percent or more above the so-called capital guidelines as desired by the OCC, OTS, FDIC, and/or the Federal Reserve System), the federal and state regulatory agencies will leave you alone. You will have a 1 on your CAMEL and/or MACRO ratings, and unless your asset quality falls out of bed, you will be ignored by your state and federal banking regulatory agencies.

Now, I know that overcapitalization is absolutely fatal for high rates of return on equity. Since most community banks and thrifts are not analyzed by bank stock analysts and do not have an organized market, this is not a significant disadvantage. As a board member, which would you rather have: a high level of capital adequacy or the FDIC on your back to raise capital? Which would you rather have: a high rate of return on equity or the ability to sleep at night? As community banks and thrifts, it is impossible to do both. I recommend to you that you have high levels of capital adequacy and keep the state and federal regulatory agencies at bay. There will be no basis for the state and federal banking regulatory agencies to be mad at you as a bank or thrift if you have levels of capital, (tangible capital and risk capital), far in excess of peer group averages. There may be a price to pay to have a lower rate of return on equity, but at the same time, the cushion that you have vis-à-vis emergencies will more than compensate for the lower return on equity.

As I travel around the country, I recommend that community banks and thrifts have a capital level at least 100 basis points higher than the peer group level. Capital adequacy is different state by state, region by region, bank by bank, or thrift by thrift. However, having a capital asset ratio 100 to 150 basis points higher than the peer group will place you in a position of comfort. You, as directors, will not have to worry about raising capital, lowering cash dividends, holding off on charging off past due, nonaccrual, or completely bad loans, nor will you have to battle the regulatory agencies as they demand that you increase capital levels at your financial institution. As I explain to bank and thrift directors throughout the country, it is worth the price of additional capital levels at your institution to be able to sleep at night and know that you are not going to be receiving any critical missives from the state and federal regulatory agencies and their district offices. Furthermore, I have never run across a bank rated below a CAMEL 2 or a MACRO 2 that had a 1 in capital adequacy. Realistically, capital 1 financial institutions usually have 1 or 2 earnings level and thus are 1 or 2 CAMEL- or MACRO-rated financial institutions. It takes effort, but the rewards are meaningful since the state and federal regulatory agencies believe that you are a competent, well-run financial institution capable of survival in this complex, uncertain marketplace.

ASSET AND LIABILITY MANAGEMENT

The performance of your bank/thrift is dependent upon the expert coordination of asset and liability management. In simple terms, this means the appropriate pricing of assets at the same time that you are pricing your deposits. Reducing banking to its simplest terms, you have to sell your assets for a price sufficiently higher than you buy your deposits and nondeposit sources of funds in order to cover your costs and make a profit. Banks and thrifts that do not have a sufficiently high net interest margin so as to remain profitable will not survive in the long run. Most of the banks and thrifts that did not survive during the 1980s died from lack of profitability, not from crooks and thieves. Asset products and deposit products must be priced at the same time and must be priced cognizant of the objective (i.e., the net interest margin desired to be obtained by the financial intermediary). Asset and liability management decisions become paramount in pricing the entire financial intermediary simultaneously. It is very similar to holistic medicine—you are not simply treating an arm or an internal problem, you are treating the entire body at the same time. Management must analyze all the factors affecting profitability simultaneously and, based upon the deposit and nondeposit flows at your bank/thrift, assets must be allocated between loans and investments and among loans and among investments in order to be priced appropriately to meet the net interest margin requirements. You as directors should be knowledgeable of asset and liability management; if you feel uncomfortable, have your outside CPA firm, inside cashier/CFO officer, or an outside consultant assist you by preparing and leading discussions and lectures on the subject until you feel comfortable and can act as checks and balances to the senior management.

Too often today the asset and liability committee (ALCO) of your bank/thrift is made up completely of inside management. That is because the directors do not feel comfortable or expert enough to be on the ALCO committee. This is a mistake because it eliminates one form of checks and balances to make sure that the pricing mechanisms are appropriate for attaining your goals and objectives. Instead of backing away from participating in asset and liability management, train several directors to be active ALCO participants. Not all directors need a Ph.D. in asset and liability management—just one will probably be more than you have now. Asset and liability management is important for the long-term profitability of your institution, and participation by your board members and senior management is essential to survivability of the bank/thrift.

RECOMMENDATIONS

- Profitability is the name of the game. Growth may be sexy, but you could fail.
- Profitability breeds capital adequacy, safety, and solvency.
- Profitability is the foundation for long-term survival.
- Significant capital adequacy keeps the regulators away—or, phrased alternatively, "capital today keeps the regulators away."
- Asset and liability management involves appropriate pricing of your asset and liability products.
- Train your directors and senior management to understand asset and liability management so that they can participate in the appropriate pricing of your products.
- Safety and solvency is conditioned upon profitability; the name of the game is to make money at your bank or thrift—not to grow like topsy.

CHAPTER 10

The Burdens of Regulation

What You Don't Know and Do May Kill You

There is so much to talk about regulation, deregulation, and the survival of the community banking institution, that it is almost impossible to figure out where to start. For years, banking and savings and loan managers, their directors, and their shareholders pushed for deregulation and elimination of federal intervention into the operations of banking institutions. Then along came the savings and loan debacle of the 1980s where two-thirds of the savings and loans in this country began to disappear, and the result was the Financial Institutions Reform, Recovery and Enforcement Act (FIRREA) in 1989. By the time the Federal Deposit Insurance Corporation Improvement Act (FDICIA) was passed in 1991, regulation was reinstated. Deregulation was dead. Deposit regulation was gone. It has been replaced by numerous burdensome administrative regulations. Banks and thrifts are more regulated today than they were in 1980, when the whole process of deregulation started. In fact, it was deregulation that killed off the savings and loan industry, and not the direct activities of the savings and loans themselves. Savings and loans ran into trouble because their cost of funds exceeded their rates of return on loans and investments, thus making them unprofitable and inadequate. The lack of profitability and capital created an environment in which Federal Home Loan Bank approval of business activities such as subdivision development, condominium development, golf course development, commercial building development, land city development, commercial lending, financial futures, swaps, and options lead to increased risk, increased unprofitability, and more rapid failure of thrifts throughout the 1980s. We all know the consequences of those activities and we know the resultant increased burdens placed upon the directors and officers of depository financial institutions by FIRREA and FDICIA. This chapter is almost analogous to the old statement "Well, in spite of that, Mrs. Lincoln, how did you enjoy the play?" You as directors and officers of community banks and thrifts are now more regulated than you were in 1980, the marketplace is far more competitive, you have far more competitors that are unregulated or quasi-regulated, and the specters of fair credit lending, the Community Reinvestment Act, and consumer compliance haunt all banks and thrifts. The burdens of regulation are real. This chapter explains their significance and how to play the game and survive.

SAFETY AND SOLVENCY REGULATIONS

One listens to the pronouncement of the state and federal banking regulators, one reads *American Banker*, *The Wall Street Journal*, and so on, one reads the articles in the various banking and savings and loan journals, and one gets the impression that the only thing that is important today is compliance with fair credit lending, the Community Reinvestment Act, and consumer-related compliance to federal laws. Interestingly, there is no less emphasis on safety and solvency when the examiners come to your door than there was before. You as directors and senior officers should be aware that safety and solvency is still the number one examination target. The only difference is that nobody talks about it anymore. There is no emphasis on it, but if you are not safe and solvent (i.e., a CAMEL 1 or 2 or a MACRO 1 or 2), you're going to be in deep doodoo with your examiners. The best way to survive as a community bank or thrift is to make sure that you are a CAMEL 1 or 2 or a MACRO 1 or 2 (these are the highest examination ratings by the bank and thrift regulatory agencies). You should have capital adequacy in excess of peer group averages, earnings in excess of peer group averages, asset quality ranked 1 or 2 by your examiners, and liquidity in excess of 25 to 35 percent. If you have all of these, your management will be graded 1 or 2. This will leave you in a position where the state and federal regulators are not concerned about your safety and solvency, and in essence, you won't have to worry about them worrying you.

Today in the mid-1990s commercial banks and thrifts are in the best financial shape they have been in decades. At the end of the first quarter in 1996, there were only 127 of the 10,000 plus BIF-member institutions on the FDIC's "problem list" (CAMELS 4 and 5). This number has declined 92 percent since 1987. Profitability in the commercial banking system has rung up five years of historically high earnings from 1991 through 1995, and past due nonaccrual and classified assets are near industry historical lows. Savings and loan profitability and capital adequacy are recovering significantly, and four years of record earnings in the banking industry have created a strong foundation for the growth of the industry for the remainder of the decade. If your bank or thrift is not a CAMEL 1 or 2 or a MACRO 1 or 2 at this time, then you have a lot of work to do in the next several years to become one. This is the best time, and if you are not a CAMEL 1 or 2 or a MACRO 1 or 2, you are in deep trouble. Safety and solvency are still the foundation for the survivability of your community bank or thrift, and reacting to the examination reports through solid remedies in order to increase your rating is the logical response to bank examinations.

THE HOT BUTTON—COMPLIANCE

Currently, the most important aspect of your examinations is compliance to state and federal rules and regulations, particularly those involving consumer credit laws, fair credit lending, and the Community Reinvestment Act. In essence, you as directors and senior officers should realize that there is almost a zero tolerance for mistakes made by your staffs in relation to filling out the forms appropriately, the granting of credit, marking such forms for home mortgage disclosure act filings (the HMDA data), filing the appropriate forms to make sure you are not discriminating against anybody under fair credit laws, rules, and regulations, and, finally, meeting the community needs of low- and moderate-income neighborhoods through the accommodation of credit on a nonarbitrary, noncapricious basis. Even though the Community Reinvestment Act, consumer compliance, and fair credit are only a part of the scope of convenience and needs (especially when mergers and acquisitions are involved), compliance issues are now the tail wagging the dog. I am not complaining about the emphasis on this subject, but as you can pretty well figure out, it is a Democratic, Clinton administration issue that has been pushed to the forefront since 1992, and may or may not be in favor after the 1996 elections. It certainly was not a significant issue during the Reagan and Bush administrations prior to 1993. As directors and officers, you should not discount the importance of compliance. If you are considered satisfactory or outstanding in terms of the compliance examinations, you will have a relatively easy ride through the remainder of this decade. If you do not rank either satisfactory or outstanding, your chances of branching, acquiring, or even surviving will be greatly affected. Even though compliance is only one factor, recent regulatory decisions as to branching, merger, holding company formation, and merger/acquisition have been denied by all of the federal regulatory agencies because of unsatisfactory compliance. This compliance deficit can either be lack of accommodation with the Community Reinvestment Act, lack of demonstrated consumer compliance through accommodation with state and federal consumer credit laws, rules, and regulations, or even challenges to the fair credit lending established by the banks and thrifts. The federal regulators are not kidding concerning compliance. This is the number one issue faced by banks and thrifts; it is the number one area of consulting for bank and thrift consultants; it is the number one discussion topic at national, state, and regional bank and thrift conferences; and it is the number one topic of conversation among bankers and thrift managers. This is not an area to discount and ignore—it can hurt you.

THE INDUSTRY HAS CHANGED

Unless you understand compliance and its significance, you are on a collision course with your state or federal regulator. I have been a bank consultant for the past 30 years, and as such have been involved in several pendulum swings in terms of regulatory examination criteria and emphasis. The major problem I run into when I work with community bank and thrift boards of directors today is their lack of acceptance or, even worse, their lack of knowledge that the industry has changed. In essence, many boards of directors have been left behind. The board of directors, including elderly senior management, may believe that they can still do things today that they could do in 1970 or even 1960. Believe me, ladies and gentlemen, you can't do things today that you did in 1995. Many of my clients over the past several years have run into problems with the Federal Reserve, comptroller of the currency, and FDIC because the president/CEO from the old school had not forced discipline on the troops within the bank to meet the new compliance standards. In spite of examination criticisms, remedial actions may not have been taken because the president/CEO really didn't believe in the new change of emphasis. Even worse, on several occasions the president/CEO convinced the board of directors that the regulatory agencies were wrong and that the criticisms were insignificant and irrelevant.

If this type of situation rings a bell in your shop, dive for cover because you are about to get bombed by one of the agencies. Over and over again I've seen the examiners win in the long run regardless of what you attempt to do. They remember year after year, examiner after examiner, and district chief after district chief. You may get rid of one bad apple, as far as you are concerned, but the next one will seem to know all about your problems with the previous one. They debrief each other better than the CIA.

What I am trying to get through to you is a very simple proposition: Compliance is the number one item on the regulator checklist these days, and any criticisms concerning your compliance accommodation must be remedied immediately without fighting city hall. If you attempt to fight city hall (i.e., take on the regulators), you are going to lose. It is not a sin to end up unsatisfactory as to consumer compliance or the Community Reinvestment Act per se. It is a sin to remain unsatisfactory and not to get off the agency's "bad list" after one unsatisfactory rating. Most financial institutions that are in trouble with the agencies are those that are fighting the system due to not understanding that the industry has changed and that we are now into a cross-t's-and-dot-i's mentality. It does you no good whatsoever to argue that the dot-the-i's-and-cross-the-t's mentality is stupid, trivial, too costly, and so on. You may be absolutely right, but your reactions are irrelevant. Here is how you stay on the good side of the regulators, whether your most recent compliance exam or CRA exam was satisfactory or not:

- Each of you as directors read the examination report front to back individually and privately.
- After the exam report has been read, sit down as a board of directors and discuss the implications of the examination report and determine what has to be done to remedy the situation.
- Meet with your president/CEO as management, not as a board member, and discuss with him or her what the problems are concerning consumer compliance, CRA, or fair credit lending.

- Establish a compliance committee at the board-of-directors level; personally I like an audit/compliance committee at community banks/thrifts since both functions can be handled by the same group of people.
- Place on the audit/compliance committee people who have the expertise to assist in remedying the deficiencies (i.e., accountants and lawyers, not farmers and housewives).
- After examining the report, determine the remedial actions required, and prioritize all remedial actions for implementation.
- Assign all remedial actions to appropriate management personnel under the authority of the president/CEO.
- Hold management accountable on at least a monthly basis by forcing management to report to the board of directors' audit/compliance committee on all remedial actions taken.
- The entire board, at least quarterly, examines all remedial actions taken and, if necessary, hires outside consultants to assist management and staff in remedying compliance examination deficiencies.
- The board of directors, if necessary, eliminates personnel who will not operate in accordance with current standards and criteria of consumer compliance.
- An objective of board of directors is to remove any deficiencies by the time of the next consumer compliance exam.

CIVIL MONEY PENALTIES AND ADMINISTRATIVE ORDERS

State and federal banking regulatory agencies are not playing games. They will give you a civil money penalty before they blink. Failure to remedy safety and solvency deficiencies, or failure to remedy compliance examination deficiencies are ample justification for civil money penalties to all board members. The board members are *expected* to supervise the management and staff and to operate in accordance with state and federal laws, rules, and regulations. One of the provisions of FIRREA in 1989 was the ability of federal regulatory agencies to remove directors and officers of newly insured depositories without due process. They can be simply suspended and/or removed by written notice, and then will have to apply for administrative hearings to be reinstated. Thus, flagrant nonconformity to consumer compliance provisions may lead to removal of directors and officers, or at least civil money penalties.

Prior to FIRREA, civil money penalties were normally not issued prior to failure by directors and officers to comply with administrative orders such as memorandums of understanding, letter agreements, or cease and desist orders. However, since FIRREA, civil money penalties have been issued against banks and thrifts when no administrative orders have been in effect. If the state or federal banking regulatory agency believes that directors and officers have acted in an unsafe and unsound manner (i.e., the bank or thrift is being subjected to unsafe and unsound banking practices), civil money penalties are promulgated against management and the directors. Consumer noncompliance is considered such an unsafe and unsound banking practice that failure to remedy the unsatisfactory conditions makes you subject to civil money penalties. Civil money penalties are promulgated based upon violations of Regulation O, lending limits to one borrower, and general failure to supervise or monitor the activities of senior management, such as failure to supervise and monitor the establishment of a branch that resulted in a cost overrun that would have won Senator William Proxmire's Golden Fleece Award. The best way to express the atmosphere today is to try to convince you that it is a total-fault system, not a no-fault system. Directors are expected to be aggressive, assertive, vigilant, and active in promoting the activities of the bank and thrift. They are expected to remedy all deficiencies as outlined by safety and solvency examinations and compliance examinations. Failure to remedy the situations that have arisen gives prima facie evidence of unsafe and unsound banking practices, and the directors are subject to discipline and/or civil money penalties. Discipline may be censure or removal; civil money penalties may be incurred without administrative orders. Do not let anybody convince you that ratings of unsatisfactory, needs to improve, or substantially noncompliant are irrelevant and insignificant. They may cost you a portion of your financial wealth if you are not on top of the situation.

In essence, comply, comply, comply. The burden of regulation is on you, and compliance lifts that burden off your back.

REGULATION WILL NOT GO AWAY

In my conversations with board members throughout the United States, I end up with the impression that board members think that regulation is going to go away. They are influenced significantly by bank and thrift presidents and senior managers who pooh-pooh regulators, chastise regulation, and discuss the insignificance of bank and thrift regulation. I wish to let you all know that as far as I'm concerned, regulation is here to stay, and we are far better off as board members and senior managers if we try to get along within the system rather than fight the system.

The purpose of regulation is to protect the public. Regulation is not all bad. Regulators are not all bad, but failure to comply with regulation is all bad.

The most appropriate approach in order to survive is to comply with regulatory pressures placed by the state and federal regulatory agencies. If we assume that regulation is here to stay, then it is least onerous to make sure that we comply with all regulations. If we attempt to fight city hall, we'll lose! On the other hand, if we spend the resources and hire the people to comply with the various rules and regulations imposed upon us, then we will survive. I realize that these individuals we hire are expensive and that they are loss leaders (i.e., cost centers rather than money makers). However, it is not our ball game; but it is the only game and we must play it within the lines.

OUTSOURCING REGULATORY COMPLIANCE

One method by which to comply with regulatory scrutiny concerning the Community Reinvestment Act, consumer compliance, fair credit, safety, solvency, and so on is to outsource the compliance and audit/examination functions of the bank/thrift. Instead of hiring and retaining one individual to act as your loan review specialist, compliance officer, security officer, or internal auditor, you can arrange with outside firms to provide such services to you on a regular basis. This trend in the 1980s was evident in the large banks and thrifts throughout the United States, but only in recent years has such outsourcing been prevalent in the community banking field. Outsourcing may become the most efficient and economical means to provide compliance and review services.[1] Outsourcing becomes a meaningful alternative to hiring individuals themselves. In addition, outsourcing has one phenomenal benefit—you get professional expertise by hiring a specialized outside consulting firm far in excess of the commercial expertise you get from one individual who attempts to be a

---

1. Christine Newkirk, "Should Banks Outsource?" *Independent Banker*, January 1996, pp. 24–26.

consumer compliance officer, loan review officer, fair credit lender, and community reinvestment officer. Many community banks and thrifts utilizing outsourcing are able to gain more expertise for less money than if they hire individuals who are part-time officers making loans, running operations, and so on and at the same time attempt to be compliance staff officers. If you want to keep your employee costs down, you have to worry about new physical space within the institution. Carefully consider outsourcing your compliance function to your audit firm or a specialized compliance firm so as to have the functions performed efficiently while not having the staffs hanging around your shop.

RECOMMENDATIONS

- Regulations are here to stay. Don't fight city hall—keep a positive spin on regulatory compliance.
- Comply, comply, comply—that is the nature of regulatory burden today.
- Be affirmative and attempt to comply as best as possible.
- Read examination reports and eliminate deficiencies.
- Form an audit/compliance committee to handle remedies and examination compliance deficiencies.
- Eliminate officers and staff who create fair credit and Community Reinvestment Act discrimination problems.
- Delegate compliance to the president/CEO and his or her staff. Hold them accountable for removing deficiencies.
- Consider outsourcing compliance so as to keep costs down with the function still covered efficiently and appropriately.
- The regulatory burden is here to stay. It may be lifted somewhat, but do not expect a significant relief—just repackaging of the regulatory burden into different forms over time.

CHAPTER 11

Utilizing Technology to Survive

Business inputs our land, labor, and capital. Banking has always been labor-intensive. Banking is now becoming capital-intensive at the expense of labor. For example, Paul Nadler in one of his columns in *American Banker* in 1994 indicated that in 1993, a full 63,000 jobs were lost at financial institutions, 25,000 of those in New York City alone. As a professor of finance for over 20 years, I train commercial bankers and thrift managers. The industry was a growth industry until the 1990s; today the industry is contracting and downsizing. Technology is the reason. Technology is crucial to your survival. However, the question is, what is technology?

Technology here involves the utilization of hardware and software to increase the bank's productivity. Change (such as computers, ATMs, point-of-sale terminals, and telephone banking) permits increased output of business units at the same or declining cost and with fewer people. Machinery may break down, but (unlike human beings) technology does not take vacations, does not request raises or fringe benefits, does not become pregnant, does not become sick, does not leave for another opportunity, and does not die or retire. As you remember, the old standard for productivity at a community bank/thrift used to be $1 million of assets per employee. Today, look at your Uniform Bank Performance Report/Uniform Thrift Performance Report and note that your peer group has over $2 million per employee. If you don't have $2 million of assets per employee today, you are behind the curve. Many of my community banking clients are now striving toward $3 million of assets per employee. This can only be achieved through increased technology and a delivery system of products and services within the community. Thus, technology is important for your survival since it permits you to increase your productivity while decreasing your labor cost per unit and over time increase your bottom line profitability.

CAVEAT—BEWARE OF SALESPERSONS

There is no area in community banking that is more replete with puffing, gregarious, fast-talking salespersons than the technology area. All you have to do is go to your state or national trade association convention and be tackled by a plethora of hardware and software salespersons. They follow you around the convention floor, they contact you in your hotel rooms, they mingle with you at receptions, and they drop by your bank after the convention is over. You can't beat them off with a stick, and that is exactly their goal. They want you to buy their hardware, their software, and their products. You can be inundated with all sorts of technological gimmicks, gadgets, and devices.

Having had my fun with the salespersons, it is important for you to shop around and determine what is available and what you need to become technologically current with the industry. Many articles in recent years have talked about how, if you are not technologically superior to your competitors, you will fail. That is utter nonsense! Many highly profitable community banks and thrifts throughout this country are slightly beyond the stage of a monk on a high stool with a quill pen and they are still earning a 2 percent rate of return on average assets. The degree of technology depends significantly on the degree of competition from other technology-oriented financial intermediaries within or on the periphery of your banking market. If you are located out in the middle of nowhere (and county seat towns are always classified as nowhere), then you are not competing against money center regional bank holding companies and branching systems, and your degree of technology within the bank or thrift is probably not as high as if you are competing with several bank holding company affiliates and a statewide branching system directly within your market. Furthermore, I am of the school that believes that three hello's and saying the person's name will win over a home computerized banking system any day. If your bank has voice mail and it takes five speech synthesizers to get where you want to within the bank, I'll lay odds that the simple receptionist at a community bank/thrift will do a far better job than the voice mail system and that type of technology will end up a burden rather than a benefit to the financial intermediary. Technology utilization by your bank/thrift is dependent upon what is necessary to deliver the services productively and efficiently within your marketplace; it is not correlated to the latest sales and marketing efforts of the country's largest hardware and software manufacturers. For example, imaging of checks and other documents is on the forefront of technology today in banking. Imaging may be of value to a multibank holding company, statewide branching system, or money center bank, but is usually not cost-efficient for a community bank/thrift. You will be inundated by salespersons boasting the benefits of imaging, and you should listen carefully to what they say, but you should undertake your own benefit–cost analysis to determine whether imaging processing within your bank/thrift is a necessity or simply a luxury toy to impress your fellow competitors within the banking market. As you are quite aware, the difference between men and boys is in the size of their toys. If you are bottom-line–conscious, then imaging or some other banking development may be of value to you 5 to 10 years from now when the cost has dropped dramatically, but it may be an expensive extra today that does not benefit your customers but certainly adversely affects your shareholders. Your purchase of technology should be based upon strong analysis, outside consulting assistance, and good common sense as to whether it is necessary at your community financial institution.

Let me give you another example. Everybody is talking today about the utilization of home-based computers to interface with bank computers in order to drive home banking delivery services to your customers. The real question is whether there is enough demand for that service within your banking market for you to spend the hundreds of thousands of dollars to provide that service to your customers. Let me give you an analogy that perhaps proves the point: I am a member of the Board of Trustees of the Toledo Society for the Blind, Inc. We provide a radio station to the visually impaired called SCAN (Sight Center Audio Network). SCAN operates on the backside of the two PBS television channels in our marketplace. SCAN may be accessed through the SAP (secondary audio programming) option on your television set. We also provide radio receivers to those who request them throughout our marketplace. We have 100 receivers out, and the manager of SCAN says that we provide this reading radio service to over 15,000 people daily. I don't believe that—I believe we are probably listened to by the same 10 to 15 people every day. In fact, I have proposed that an announcement be made at various times over a three-day period saying that the first 10 people who hear the announcement should call in and receive $25 cash. That would mean we would give away $750 cash. I believe that we would be out less than $100. The annual budget for SCAN is about $60,000 per year, including personnel and a whole group of volunteers who read on our behalf. We purchase radio shows from the radio reading services throughout the country plus national public radio. We provide a valuable service, but we are probably losing our tail feathers on this service. Why? Because the demand for that service is far less than the cost we expend on an annual basis to provide that service. If you do the same, then it is a loss leader to your bank/thrift, and you must consciously provide that service knowing that it is a loss leader. Another loss leader you may have is the trust department; you may consciously continue the trust department knowing that overall it may provide a foundation for other services offered. However, technology should be analyzed for the benefit of the service to your total productivity, not simply because home computerized banking is "hot" and you should provide that service because one or two customers want it. You cannot provide 100 percent of the services 100 percent of your customers want. You have to make a business decision on which services you can provide at an expense less than the return for such service. For example, if you estimate that only 15 people within your community would utilize a system that interfaces their home computers with your bank-based computer or data service provider computer, then it might not be worthwhile to provide that service for just 15 people. On the other hand, if that service would be used by 200 people comprising 50 percent of your highest average balance depositors, then that service becomes almost a necessity, certainly more than a luxury. You have to make that decision, but only after you have done enough analysis to determine whether it is cost-effective.

INTERNAL COMPUTERIZATION AND/OR OUTSOURCING

The first real question for the community bank/thrift is whether the basic processing computers should be internal or provided through a service bureau. This is not a one-time decision. Even if you have brought the computers inside, they become obsolete, and the decision becomes a new decision as to whether to replace the computers or go outside. Again, this is a benefit–cost analysis problem. One significant barrier to outside data service processors in the past has been the inflexibility of the reports received by the financial institution. This has been remedied by the ability to download the data on network PCs within the bank/thrift, so today it is no longer a barrier. Furthermore, outside processing frees up room within the financial institution and lowers employee costs. This may be an excellent trade-off for paying the charges.

The degree of computerization within the bank/thrift is critical. My clients run the gamut from banks with almost no PCs to those that are networked, one for every employee except perhaps the janitor. I am talking about computers that network the tellers to the backroom as well as the loan officers to the teller and the customer service representatives (CSRs) to the loan officers, and so on. In this type of system, e-mail can go to all employees of the bank at one time; individuals in offices many miles apart can be in touch by computer with each other instantaneously. On the other hand, your institution may not need that degree of networking, but it's coming. Every one of your employees who needs a computer should have one; if they do not have one, you are behind the curve—and falling farther behind quickly.

The most important reason for having technology within the bank/thrift is to comply with all of the detailed regulations that are currently in vogue. Without a loan operational system, you are going to make significant mistakes in preparing loan applications, processing loans, documenting all aspects of the loan, and preparing data for the various federal regulatory agencies concerning the Community Reinvestment Act, HMDA, and so on. If human beings won't do this properly, computers will. Thus, computerization of your loan functions is vital to proper compliance. Besides, from this computerization you learn an awful lot about what is going on in your financial institution—if you run across a problem that raises regulatory flags, you can remedy the situation before the examiners arrive. Utilization of computerization to handle your loan application and operational functions diminishes chances of making compliance errors that will come back to haunt you at a later time. Moreover, these loan operations systems are far more efficient than handwriting the applications and the documents, and this type of technology increases the productivity of the department.

PRODUCTIVITY VERSUS COST

As board members of community banks and thrifts you should be concerned about technology sweeping through your institution in order to increase productivity without increasing cost. As noted earlier, technology can be more cost-efficient than human beings. ATM machines operate 24 hours a day, seven days a week, and do not go on vacation or get sick. Unfortunately, ATM machines break down, so we certainly hope the service person is not on vacation or sick. The ATM machine can provide 95 percent of the ordinary services provided by your financial institution. Point-of-sale terminals, which are being implemented currently, can add another element to the service of merchant business throughout the country while at the same time providing debit card service to your customer. Just make sure as board members that the technology you are adding is cost-effective. In essence, make sure you keep asking the question, If we don't get this piece of hardware or software, are we placing ourselves at a competitive disadvantage? Are the other financial institutions in the market providing a service using this technology? Are we simply trying to keep up with the Joneses (or, in banking terms, with the Bank Ones or Nations Banks or City Banks), or will this new loan operational system provide us with the ability to process 50 percent more loans with one fewer person? These are the important questions that must be asked rather than simply adding technology for technology sake. You should listen carefully when your president/CEO or (horrors of horrors) your vice president for operations—known around the bank as "geek" or "nerd"—proposes new technology. You are not there to reward them, but reward your employees for increased productivity through technology.

My point here is that the board of directors usually reviews technology proposals and rolls over and plays dead. This is simply because the board of directors knows very little about technology. Therefore, if you don't know anything about it, you take at face value what your president/CEO or other senior management people say. That is a good way to go to the poor farm—buy equipment and software of no real value, and make long-term earnings less than they should be, while at the same time not increasing productivity and efficiency at your financial institution.

Every board has at least one member who is now a computer whiz. It's almost enough to make you nauseous when you do strategic planning retreats. There is always one director, always retired, who now knows more about computers than Bill Gates and Steve Jobs combined. This individual gets up in the morning, drinks coffee, and plays on the Internet all day long until he has to go off to an incontinency test or go over to the Moose Lodge to beat on other veterans from bygone wars. If there is anything worse than relying upon the president and the vice president for operations, it's letting your computer expert on the board take over what technology you need. You put those three together and you will end up looking like a radar station in the Antarctic rather than a commercial bank in Nebraska. Common sense should prevail. (Do others have the same type of technology? How much did it cost them? Let's talk to them and find out whether it is working. Would they continue to use it or would they love to get rid of it?) These are the kind of commonsense questions that should be asked because you are spending good shareholders' money and may be increasing expenditures at the expense of profitability. You should have very good reasons why you do what you do.

RECOMMENDATIONS

- Plan ahead for hardware and software purchases and keep them under control.
- Compare your technological needs to competitors'.
- Determine the demand for the services provided through technology. Don't just provide everything because one or two people want it.
- Determine what outside data processors can do, vis-à-vis internal computerization and providing technological products and services.
- Force management to justify the utilization of technology. It's not just toys for the president and the vice president of operations to play with.
- Become informed as board members of what technology should be added and what should be ignored—do your homework as board members. The purpose of technology is to increase productivity and efficiency while at the same time reducing employee costs.
- Provide technology to improve compliance through increasing confirmation and conformance with compliance technicalities in all applications and documentation forms.

CHAPTER 12

What Services
Do We Need?

The last time you trotted out to a state or national convention, speakers were touting new banking products and services that would guarantee your survival as a community bank/thrift. If you just sold insurance, sold mutual funds and annuities, provided secondary mortgage market services, and so on, you would survive as a community bank or thrift, thanks to their help. I am not impressed by this type of hype and puffing, and I hope you are not either. Some of these services are completely legitimate and may assist you in providing services to your public. None of these services is so essential that if you don't sell mutual funds, you'll die. This chapter may be short in terms of length, but it is vital. Here I hope to express to you the importance of understanding what products and services sell within your community and market and which ones are nothing more than window dressing, loss leaders, and bombs in your portfolio.

KNOW YOUR DEMAND

As a financial institution consultant, I wander through banks and thrifts all over the country. My impression of how services are provided is based on two factors: (1) historical tradition and (2) whatever new product or service tickled the fancy of the president. I am convinced that no scientific market research was done as to what the marketplace demanded in terms of products and services. First, historical tradition is great, but it simply means that banks and thrifts don't throw any products and services away. Answer me honestly—when was the last time you dropped a service out of your product portfolio? An awful lot of my clients say, "Never. We are providing new products, but we don't get rid of the old ones even if they are not in demand anymore." Second, the president's ideas of what will make a good product and service may be absolutely correct or 100 percent incorrect, but without knowing what the customers within the marketplace want, you'll never know. Your new products and services provided by your financial institution should be based upon scientific market research on what is needed within the marketplace, who is supplying it, and what niches are available for you to provide that product and service at a profit.

REMEMBERING PROFITABILITY

Remember that old joke about losing money on every item sold, but making it up on volume? As board and senior management members, you should make sure that you are not providing products and services that are losing money unit by unit, but you are hoping to make it up on volume. You probably have one or two of those services—try your trust department. Almost all trust departments at community banks and thrifts are unprofitable. Most of them have not made money for years and most community banks cannot compete with the big money center metropolitan trust departments. Having a trust department is more a matter of tradition and ego than it is common sense. Recently a bank with a $3 million trust department decided to determine what it could to become a major player. The bottom line was that it should sell off it's trust department and try to be a major player in another field of endeavor. It was surrounded by multibillion-dollar trust departments with hundreds of employees, yet this small bank was attempting to increase its trust department with one officer and one secretary. The ambitions were not in line with the realities. That's all we are talking about here—realities. If you are 50 to 100 years behind others in developing a trust department, then don't beat your head against the wall—find some way that you can be 50 to 100 years ahead of somebody else, and take advantage of it. For example, one small bank in northern Ohio about 20 years ago became a major financier of general aviation airplanes from all over the country. Its portfolio was not diversified—there were an awful lot of airplane loans, but there were an awful lot of airplane loans all the way from California to New York and Florida to Maine. This bank was known throughout the industry as one that financed airplanes. It found a niche and did something better than anybody else in the country. You can do that within your marketplace, although perhaps not as dramatically.

Remember profitability at all times. You are not running a charity, regardless of what the regulators tell you. Even if you are a mutual savings and loan or mutual savings bank and you are reading this book, you are not running a charity. You are running a mutually owned business that has to make profits in order to build up reserves in case of emergencies from bad lending or improper investing. You should be just as profitability-oriented as the commercial bank down the street with 500 shareholders. Profitability is the name of the game, and your products and services should provide profitability rather than be loss leaders. You can barely afford one loss leader. Why try five or six? If the product doesn't make you money—and functional cost analysis will provide the information to you—then dump the sucker. Either operate without it or supplement it with something else.

THE BASICS OF BANKING

You do not need to provide every banking product and service that the largest money center, multibank holding company and statewide branching financial institution in your marketplace offer. You can survive without attempting to keep up with the Joneses when you do not have the wherewithal, the market research, the advertising, or the marketing to do so. You can survive with basic banking products and services.

Let me give you an example: There is a bank in Toledo, Ohio, called Capital Bank, N.A. Capital Bank was started in August 1989 after raising $13.2 million in capital. As of year-end 1995, it had assets in excess of $483 million, with a total equity capital of $36.1 million. The bank has been profitable from the very start, primarily due to the $13 million in capital. But the point of my example is that it offers only basic banking. It provides checking accounts, NOW accounts, a multitiered savings product, and certificates of deposit. It provides extensive commercial lending products along with minor mortgage and consumer installment products to those who are the basic customers of the bank. It operates from one office and has all employees with cellular phones in their cars to act as couriers and salespersons while they are out of the bank. It does not provide mutual funds, annuities, insurance, and trust powers. It leaves all of those to others who have been in the business for a long time. It provides basic banking and has gone from zero deposits on August 23, 1989, to over $437 million in deposits in one office by the end of 1995. It must have done something right. The answer is quite simple: It charges less for loans and pays more for deposits so people show up. As paraphrased from *Field of Dreams*, "If it's priced right, they will come."

Thus, if your bank or thrift has a basic range of products that are priced appropriately, then you can survive regardless of what kind of products are thrown at you by the "big boys." Sure, there are going to be some customers who want fancy computerized home banking or even mutual funds or annuities through your banking office. There are always going to be baby boomers, yuppies, and X-generation people who are not satisfied by your basic banking products and services. However, most of your customers will be thrilled with good pricing even if it is a simple product.

QUALITY SERVICE

First of all, it is absolutely true that if you have a quality product, selling it with quality service is an outstanding way to provide the product to the public. However, it is also true that if you do not have a quality product, quality service can still sell the product to the public for a long time before anybody catches on. I am not implying that your bank or thrift should attempt to sell an inferior product, but I sure know that if you don't have quality service through your personnel, even a quality product will not sell.

What the surveys have indicated is that people who deal with financial institutions want quality service. They want to be known by name and they want personalized, efficient service when they are in your financial institution or at the drive-in window. They want to be treated as an individual and want to be treated in an enlightened, educational, intellectual manner. They do not want to be talked down to, or considered dummies; they want you to explain exactly what is going on vis-à-vis their loan or deposit functions with your institution. All this can be done with basic products and services; you don't have to worry about providing them with property and casualty insurance or real estate brokerage just to keep them within the bank or thrift for basic services. If you provide them quality service, excellent hours of operation, convenient locations, and an environment where they are pleased to do business with you, you can probably get by with minimal products and services supplied by excellent personnel.

FITTING YOUR PRODUCTS WITH YOUR PERSONNEL

I have been a community banking consultant for almost 30 years. As I consult with my clients nationwide and talk to bankers and thrift managers throughout the country at professional presentations, I find that most products and services provided by the community banking organization are based upon the talents, or lack of same, of the personnel within the financial institution. We assume that once you have performed a market analysis of what products and services are needed within your community, you should then provide those products and services by retraining your current personnel, and, if necessary, either replacing or adding new personnel who have the talent necessary to provide such products and services. As an illustration, let us assume there is a substantial need for residential mortgage lending within your market, and you wish to place the heavy volume of residential mortgage loans into the secondary market rather than keep them within your own portfolio. Unfortunately, you don't have any personnel who are expert in secondary mortgage lending, especially the applications and operations of same. The old process was to simply ignore the secondary market. I am suggesting that you enter the secondary mortgage market actively by either retraining your current personnel, adding new personnel that have the expertise, or replacing current personnel with new personnel who have the expertise. You can no longer afford the luxury of having personnel on your staff who are not capable of meeting the modern needs of banking. If your staff can't cut it, cut them. You need personnel who can be flexible, trainable, and positive in their viewpoint of providing the products and services to the public that they desire. On a regular basis, I run across community banks and thrifts whose personnel is so fixed in their own mind as to how things should be done, and often have no clue how things are done at other financial institutions, that they are an impediment to the provision of quality products and services. If you plan to survive as a community banking institution and compete with expert personnel at the larger national and state-oriented institutions, you have to provide quality service at your financial institution. You cannot do so with Neanderthal personnel. You have to replace the dinosaurs with cyberspace junkies. You have to provide the service through quality personnel. Either retraining or replacement may be necessary for you to provide those products and services.

COMPENSATION, COMMISSIONS, AND COMMITMENT

Many of the new products available to your financial institution are commission-oriented. For example, the sale of insurance, the sale of mutual funds and annuities, and the provision of tax preparation services and credit bureau services are not traditional salary-oriented services provided by a commercial bank or thrift. We are so traditionally oriented, we pay salaries and possibly bonuses to our employees. The types of services that we can provide into the future are going to be commission-oriented. Perhaps we need to look for fewer accountants and finance people and more marketing, English, and history majors. Bankers have always felt that they had to be above the "sales" culture as noted in Chapter 8. The provision of these new products and services are best accomplished through incentive compensation, commissions, and bonuses rather than by simply paying the person's salary. Thus, we should promote incentive compensation for the provision of these new nonbanking but closely related services. You must pay people what they are worth, and fire them when they are not worth anything.

You should set up a separate division for the sale of these new services that are closely related to banking services. These people may not be the old professional banker, and they do not need to be trained in commercial banking schools or receive the educational background of the traditional banking services. They need to be supervised by a sales manager and taught sales skills. They must be marketing-oriented, gregarious, outgoing, hard-working people who don't worry about banking hours. Many of your bank's or thrift's services will be provided outside of banking hours. Insurance salespeople do more work in the evenings and on weekends than they do during business hours. Real estate salespeople work more on weekends than they do during the week. Securities salespeople work not only during the office hours but also afterward as they do telemarketing.

Not only do they work strange hours, they often look different. These types of salespeople hustling your closely related banking services will be wearing sport coats rather than suits, and dresses rather than suits. They will be wearing Nike and Adidas rather than wingtips and pumps. Furthermore, they will be seen more frequently outside the bank or thrift than inside. In fact, they won't be making any money if they are sitting around waiting for your customers to come in. They will be seen in local restaurants, bars, country clubs, and marinas and they will be actively involved in the country club set, snowmobiling, sailboat racing, local stockcar races, rodeos, and economic development groups. These are going to be outside salespersons selling commission-oriented services of your institution, and if they are trained well, they are going to refer these alternative investment clients to your bank or thrift for basic business services.

Money—oh, is that a sore subject. There is a very good chance that your outstanding salespeople will outearn most of the banking professionals within your shop. If you are going to succeed in selling closely related banking services, they must make a very good living through their efforts. This is why I recommend that you slip them off into a division of their own so that interfacing with the professional bankers may be less onerous. If they are earning more money for themselves, then they are earning more money for the bottom line of the bank or thrift. It is a win–win situation, and if your professional bankers don't like it, fire them. These types of services are the wave of the future, and if you want to survive in your community, you have got to provide the services desired. If the typical loan officer or operations guru is not happy about the money being made by the flashy salespeople over in the 4(c)(8) division, then give him a very strong lecture on how to fly right, since he can be replaced by somebody else who doesn't have the same hang-ups. A short reminder that bankers are in excess supply may be an advantage to your lecture. This problem is a reflection of different industries combining at one company. Insurance companies, securities firms, and real estate firms have always paid based upon the productivity of their employees (at least the salespeople). Commercial banks and thrifts have not. If you combine the services of the insurance, real estate, and securities industries with those of the banking industry, there are going to be problems, but a strong board of directors' dictate and strong management implementation of the new salary and commission arrangements can increase profitability to the institution.

SUPERMARKET BANKING

Supermarket banking is a perfect illustration of the new wave of product and service delivery systems that are completely unfamiliar to traditional banking. Not too long ago at a board meeting, after they had applied for and received approval for a supermarket branch, the directors were deciding which of the tellers to take out of the main office and send down to the supermarket branch. This Neanderthal thinking is illustrative of what can happen if one doesn't understand the new banking brought on by new cultures and mores. The type of people needed at the supermarket branch were entirely different than the professional staff at the main office. Fortunately, nobody was transferred from the main office to the supermarket branch. We took salespeople and taught them banking, rather than vice versa. The supermarket branch has been very successful because it's not a traditional bank—it would have been a flaming disaster if we had utilized bankers. Proper ambiance (including the proper personnel) is just as important as the right location. You wouldn't consciously have a male salesperson selling women's flimsy negligees at Victoria's Secret. Similarly, you wouldn't have an accountant selling banking services at your supermarket branch. The success of your supermarket branch depends upon the quality of personnel, and the quality of personnel depends upon the type. They must be willing to work long hours, solicit business from people who have no idea who they are, and be a type A extrovert. With those kinds of people, your supermarket branch can be a success as one of your new services provided to meet the needs of the public.

PRODUCTS AND SERVICES TO CONSIDER

Some of the products and services noted below are premised on the cost analysis as to whether they are worthwhile to offer or not. You should (or must) have done a market research study to determine the cost benefits of the products and/or services to be offered, or to determine the appropriateness of retaining the products/services currently being offered. Moreover, you must have determined that your staff will not be able to handle the additional pressure and sales effort.

INSURANCE POWERS

Insurance powers for community banks are in flux. In some states, community banks and thrifts may offer a full range of insurance services. In other states, they may only offer property and casualty insurance and, in some jurisdictions, only credit life. For areas with populations of less than 5,000 people, national banks can operate full-service life, property, and casualty insurance agencies. If your bank or thrift is capable of offering insurance, examine the issue and provide the service. If you can't, keep watching—sooner or later you will be able to. The trend is toward insurance powers for depository financial institutions. Do not be dissuaded by the argument that you'll lose the insurance agents' accounts in your town. So what! They have the gall and the audacity to offer a full-range of depository services now. The major insurance companies have their own commercial banks. They offer mortgage services, commercial banking services, and certificates of deposit or their equivalent. They offer financial planning. When was the last time anyone who was a CFP or a CFHC ever recommended your bank or thrift as a source of investment? The only reason you will not compete against insurance companies and insurance agencies is that you have an insurance agent on the board and he or she screams like bloody murder. I have the answer to that: Shoot the director! You should remove the director and start competing. Obviously another tack is to buy out the insurance agent and make her a part of your bank or bank holding company subsidiary. In many local communities the *only* exit vehicle for the local insurance agents would be a buyout by a local community bank or thrift. The sons and daughters are off to the big city and have moved 3,000 miles away. Nobody else in the insurance agency wants to run it or can afford to purchase it from the principals. Therefore, you enter as the white knight and buy them out. On the other hand, they can help you out since they know something about insurance and you have no one in the bank who knows the difference between a life insurance policy and a property and casualty policy. It's a win–win situation! They are able to sell out over a period of time (i.e., the buyout is based upon earnings), and at the same time you provide them with continued employment and a livelihood until they decide to retire fully.

Insurance is a natural. If you do not follow up on this power, a significant product and service in the community will be eliminated and you will suffer.

SECURITIES POWERS

I am lumping discount brokerage as well as the sale of mutual funds and annuities under the same subheading. I have yet to run across a community bank or thrift that has discount brokerage powers that has honestly told me it is making any money. The best explanation is that it isn't losing the customers that give it the discount brokerage business.

The financial institution might lose significant business if it did not offer discount brokerage, although the total volume of same may not provide for net profits.

The sale of mutual funds and annuities is entirely different than the sale of depository products. First of all, to sell mutual funds and annuities, one must be registered with the SEC and pass tests from the National Association of Securities Dealers. In contrast, bankers are totally untested. There are no requirements to pass tests sponsored by the Federal Deposit Insurance Corporation, Office of the Comptroller of the Currency, Office of Thrift Supervision, and so on. Furthermore, bank personnel cannot sell depository services and mutual funds and annuities at the same time. You have to separate the functions. However, separating the functions is no big deal. You simply have two crews: one selling depository products and one selling mutual funds and annuities.

Mutual funds and annuities are a distinct product line and should be added to your overall products, but they are not substitutes for current products—they are additional products and services. There is no risk of loss for a principal certificate of deposit (as long as it is under $100,000), but there is a possibility of loss to bond and equity mutual funds. Furthermore, it doesn't cost your customers a dime to take out a certificate of deposit or a passbook or open up a checking account (except for the cost of checks), but a front-load fee is often charged with mutual fund purchases and there may be a 12B-1 annual marketing and management fee to sustain the mutual fund. Mutual funds and annuities are appropriate for some customers but not for others. Having determined that mutual funds are a good product for the community, you might offer them, but only at the risk of incurring liability for inappropriate sale and solicitation of mutual funds.

The real question today is whether you should (1) sell the mutual funds yourself, (2) contract with a firm that will sell mutual funds and annuities for you by supplying a person to sell such, or (3) contract with a registered brokerage house that will place an office within your facilities. All of these are being done currently by financial institutions throughout the United States. I have seen no survey of the results of the differing approaches to the sale of mutual funds and annuities. I don't even have a scientific random sample of my own clients to determine which method works better. My clients tell me that all three work and all three don't work. You are going to have to do your own homework and find out which provider of mutual funds and annuities services you want to utilize, or whether you want to have a regional brokerage firm within your shop or else simply do it yourself. Network with competitors and colleagues to find out which works in their shops and which will work in yours. The wrong provider will sink the whole effort.

As with the other new services discussed in this chapter, I should probably note that the two banking national trade associations (the American Bankers Association and the Independent Bankers Association of America) as well as the America's Community Bankers (the former Savings and Community Bankers of America) have subsidiaries as well as certified vendors that can assist you in providing these services. In addition, many state-affiliated trade associations have vendors that are certified within your state to provide such mutual fund and annuity sales programs. You should determine which of these vendors is of value to you. Don't hesitate to review several, and compare and contrast their services through cross-reference with competitors and colleagues.

TAX PREPARATION AND FINANCIAL PLANNING

Community banks and thrifts are permitted to provide financial advice, investment advice, financial planning, and tax preparation for their clients. These are products and services within communities that may be of great assistance to the customers of the financial institutions. Most of your customers believe that you are financial leaders and have the expertise to provide these kind of services. Through a subsidiary of a bank or thrift holding company or through the trust department of your institution, you can provide these services in direct competition with CPA firms, private tax preparers, and individual financial planners. Remember, they take no prisoners. Why should you?

LEASING AND FACTORING

Leasing and factoring are two sophisticated forms of commercial lending that can be utilized by community banks and thrifts to provide an additional service. Many banks and thrifts simply do not provide leasing and factoring services since they don't have the expertise within the staff. Hire the expertise and solve your problem. These services are needed in almost every marketplace. If you don't believe me, just take a look at the UCC filings from your county and determine how many different firms are doing leasing and factoring operations within your county and filing

UCC 1's in direct competition with the leasing and factoring you could do. There is no reason why you could not be in this market.

RECOMMENDATIONS

- Research your banking market to determine what products and services are needed by your customers.
- Provide products and services that are needed. Forget about those that look catchy and are being provided by someone else.
- Eliminate products and services that are loss leaders; concentrate on those that make a profit.
- Provide only those products and services that your staff is capable of handling. If they don't have the expertise, either train them or fire them.
- The basic banking products and services are critical for your survival. The closely related banking services are the frosting on the cake, not the cake batter itself.

CHAPTER 13

Community Bank Survival and the Board of Directors

If you don't survive as a community bank or thrift, it will be your fault—yes, you, the directors. Your shareholders will sue you, the regulatory agencies will sue you, and, even worse, the professional litigative plaintiffs who own one share of your stock sponsored by sleazy plaintiff law firms throughout the United States will sue you. Your jobs as directors are difficult, and they have been made more difficult by the passage of FIRREA in 1989 and FDICIA in 1991. Prior to 1989, in spite of corporate tradition that boards of directors ran financial institutions, in most cases the management ran the institutions and the board of directors were simply a *Last Supper* painting. Remember back to when you've had your picture taken for the Annual Report—you're all standing in a line or sitting at a table perusing reports and you all look like a *Last Supper* painting. Those days are gone. Commencing in 1989, the environment changed for directors of community banks and thrifts. You are now expected to be proactive, vigilant, and assertive, and you are going to be held responsible for being in charge of the financial institution that you serve. You can no longer say that you relied upon the president/CEO or other senior officers in doing your job. They are going to be allowed to say that they relied on you, because you are the last stop before oblivion. As Harry Truman's sign said, **The buck stops here.** That is exactly your role as board members. You have the corporate power to supervise or monitor the bank or thrift, and in doing so make sure that it is safe and solvent.

Realistically, you can hire outside legal, accounting, loan review, credit review, Community Reinvestment Act, consumer compliance, fair lending, internal control, and other consultants and authorities to assist you to make sure that the bank is safe and solvent. If you don't do so, you will be held liable for the failure and/or poor performance of the bank or thrift.

The purpose of this chapter is not to explore once again the duties and responsibilities of bank and thrift directors. This has been done repeatedly—recently by one of my own publications.[1] The purpose of this chapter is to assist you in developing techniques to improve the performance of your bank or thrift so that it (1) remains safe, solvent, profitable, and capitally adequate and (2) meets the demands and needs of the shareholders (members) in terms of rates of return on investment. In this chapter, we develop techniques by which you as the members of the board of directors perform your duties so as to provide the leadership necessary for the management and staff to implement the policies and procedures that result in a profitable, safe, solvent financial intermediary.

FIRST TECHNIQUE FOR SURVIVAL: BE IN CHARGE

The most important thing you can do as a board of directors is to be in charge of the bank or thrift. You should tell the president and his/her staff what to do. You should be comfortable enough as directors that (1) you understand the trend of the industry, the condition of the bank or thrift, and the projected performance of your institution and (2) you're able to tell your management and staff what you want them to do on your behalf. This is what you are expected to do, and this is the best technique for survival. If you sit back, fall asleep, or pay no attention to what the management is doing, you will pay the price. If, on the other hand, you are in charge, hire and maintain the best management possible (see the next chapter), and make sure that the staff does the job professionally, then your institution will have outstanding rates of return on assets and equity, and be a financial leader in the community. In essence, what I am saying is that you are responsible for what goes on—if you sit there and think that you just have a part-time job, forget it!

---

1. Douglas V. Austin, *Financial Institution Director Liabilities and Responsibilities*, 4th edition (Toledo, Ohio: Austin Financial Services, Inc., 1996).

BANK DIRECTORS' DUTIES AND COMPENSATION

As board members, you are absolutely in charge of the institution, and it must not fail. Your duties are universal, but your director's fees are local and subject to question. Section 132[2] of FDICIA permits the FDIC and other federal regulatory agencies to second guess the amounts of fees, honoraria, and fringe benefits that you receive as directors. I think I understand the reason for that: They don't want you to make hundreds of thousands of dollars as directors as the financial institution is failing. On the other hand, if you note most of the litigation that arose from the savings and loan debacle of the 1980s, it was inside management/ directors who were sued for making hundreds of thousands of dollars or more, and the outside directors were sued simply because they were there. Yes, there were occasions where outside directors made a fortune or were alleged to have made a fortune, but these cases were minuscule in relationship to those of inside managers and officers. Thus, I wouldn't lose sleep over the fact that someone is looking over my shoulder. However, I would set up a system by which the results of my bank/thrift would be the foundation for my income as a director. For example, if my bank is equal to incomes at peer group banks, then my income as a director should be equal to peer group banks. On the other hand, if my bank/thrift has a rate of return on assets (forget equity because of all the comments made earlier in this book) 25 percent above peer group averages, then its board of directors deserves 25 percent more than peer group averages. The same is true for rates of return on assets, CAMEL 1 ratings, and outstanding ratings in both Community Reinvestment Act and consumer compliance, which prompt higher salaries and fees. One subject that is not a topic of this book is director compensation per se, and I must just quickly mention that I am not in favor of stock options for directors since I don't think they are in a position to earn them. I strongly believe in stock options for management (see the next chapter), but for directors I think this is a red herring. You should be paid current income or deferred compensation equal to your results as directors; stock options make no sense to bank or thrift directors because it is not that type of a business and you do not participate daily in the operations that make the results.

2. Public Law 102-242 (December 19, 1991), Section 132(c), Standards for Safety and Soundness, Compensation Standards; 105 State. 2268; 12 USC 1831.

Thus, as directors, you should be paid based upon your results. However, if you want an inkling of how much you are worth, please see Table 13–1, which shows the amount of money you should receive as directors of community banks/thrifts, based upon asset size. You will note that this chart is not broken down between current compensation (such as actual cash) and deferred compensation (such as compensation received after you retire and insurance policies). Furthermore, it is not broken down to indicate that some directors receive health benefits, country club memberships, bank cards, and so on. The table indicates the amount of compensation to be received, in all forms, by directors based upon asset size. As far as I am concerned, this is a minimum. If you have a problem paying this amount to your directors, slice the number of board members from nine to five, and pay them. Considering the amount of the liability of your board, this is actually a pittance per year. You are expected to spend your time, resources, and effort, and go to conventions, seminars, and workshops in return for which you get $500 a month!

Alternatively phrased, as a member of the board of directors of a community bank/thrift you should be paid at least as much as your local attorney will ask for a retainer in case you get into trouble. If you consider $6,000 to be an ample retainer, then you're not going to a very good attorney. There is no reason why you shouldn't be paid between $750 and $1,500 a month for your efforts on behalf of the bank/thrift, and if you are not being paid this type of consideration, you can probably go out and sell Avon products or go door to door for Amway more profitably than you can be a director. As you are quite aware, you cannot eat status.

BUYING AND MAINTAINING MANAGEMENT

This is just a cursory paragraph. I am going to discuss management competency and compensation in the next chapter. However, I have got to get you warmed up for the discussion. Too often directors believe that management is a necessary evil. You have to have management or the place won't run. Furthermore, many directors believe that the president/CEO should only be paid $60,000-$70,000 because nobody else in the county makes any more than that. Too often the board of directors doesn't pay attention to peer group salary levels, merit evaluations, or competitive conditions in determining management salaries. The best line of defense in your bank/thrift is the quality of your

TABLE 13-1

Range of Director Compensation by Size of Institution

Under $50 million	$5,000–$7,500
$50–$100 million	$7,500–$10,000
$100–$150 million	$10,000–$15,000
Over $150 million	Over $15,000

management. If you fail to realize that, you will lose in the long-run because incompetent management will cause you more problems than you can solve.

SECOND TECHNIQUE:
HIRE COMPETENT MANAGEMENT

As outlined in the preceding subsection, management is essential to the survival of your community bank/thrift. However, you have to hire the best management, not just management. Furthermore, you have to compensate them properly, and you have to give them stock options (phantom stock), fringe benefits, country club memberships, bank cards, and so on since they are the most important people who protect your liability as directors. Senior management is the most crucial aspect of your community bank/thrift. The next chapter details how to compensate competent management.

STRATEGIC PLANNING:
KNOW WHERE YOU ARE GOING

As Chapter 3 said, strategic planning is key to the survival of a community bank/thrift. You as the board of directors are responsible for determining the future course of the bank/thrift. This chapter's purpose is to explain how to perform your duties so as to survive as a community banking institution; I'm simply reiterating in this paragraph the importance of strategic planning and knowing where you are going as a financial intermediary in order to survive. If you simply operate day-to-day, don't care about where the institution is in 20 years, don't care about whether you make a profit, or don't care whether your shareholders make a fair rate of return on their investment, then you won't survive. Since your purpose is to survive, and you can if you do your job right, then strategic planning becomes critical to your survival path.

BOARD OF DIRECTOR EDUCATION

You as board members are expected to understand the trends of the industry, problems faced by the industry and the financial institutions therein, and problems faced by your management and staff. If you've spent no time being educated concerning banking in the past five years, then you are probably typical of the average director. Board of director education is essential. It doesn't all have to be national conventions, or proprietary seminars throughout the United States. In Chapter 15, we shall discuss in detail board of director and management education. Here I am just pointing out that you must remain educated to do your job properly. Each day you go to work as an outside director doing something professionally, and you try to be as good as you possibly can in order to make a living for your family, provide funds for your retirement, and be an asset to your community. On the other hand, if you show up at the board meetings completely uneducated, not up to snuff as to what is going on in your community concerning banking, and with no clues about what is going on in the economy concerning financial matters, then you are not doing your job professionally. Almost all of you are not professional bankers and financiers. Most of you are in any other field except that. You must concentrate on outside board of director education in order to be able to act as a supervisor and monitor of what goes on within your financial institution in order to make sure that the bottom doesn't fall out of the bucket.

RECRUITMENT, RETENTION, AND REMOVAL OF DIRECTORS

The board of directors has to be as strong as possible. You as a board member should be surrounded by the best people possible within your community. People should not be on your board of directors because they were born to someone who was previously on the board, or are friends of the president, or have lots of money and bought their way on the board. Board members should be placed on the board because of expertise, experience, common sense, honesty, integrity, veracity, and the ability to serve. You are only as strong as your weakest link, and some boards have very weak links. You should leave the board of directors when you are no longer interested in performing the job, are out of town extensively because of retirement or business, or have become mentally or physically incapable of doing the job. You should have directors who disagree but are not disagreeable. They should be prepared and they should vote their conscience based upon informed decisions. If they simply show up to collect their fees and find being on the board of directors "fun," you should help them resign. Directorships seem to be life career opportunities. You may not be able to keep your job on a regular basis in town, but you can stay on the board of directors until you die. This has got to stop. If you don't perform, you should be removed. If you perform, you can stay there forever. Mandatory retirement ages are anachronous. People do not become senile automatically at 65 or 70. Some people are senile at 40 and some never become senile. Some add quality to the board of directors until they fall over, and some never once have any socially redeemable business value. The only way your board can be strong enough to provide the leadership necessary to keep the financial institution surviving is to have the best people possible within the community performing the duties of directors. If the individuals are not attentive, participative, prepared, or consistent in their attendance, they should be given the best farewell party you can afford. Realistically, you can't afford to keep them around. Besides, some of the older directors start to suffer from Bankheimers, a degenerative disease that has the symptom of saying that all decisions should be made under the conditions of what banking was like 20 years ago. Bankheimers is a disease that has no cure, and usually results in the death of the financial institution. Directors should contribute 100 percent or else leave the board and stay at home dribbling and watching television.

MOTIVATING THE MANAGEMENT

It is an essential function of the board of directors to motivate the management to perform at a level far beyond and above their normal proficiency. This can be done through role conjoining, written policy statements, threats of employment termination, but most frequently and most effectively through the provision of quality remuneration, fringe benefits, and the opportunity to excel as management. Since the management will often outlive the tenure of individual directors, it is up to the directors to provide the foundation for future solid financial performance of the financial institution; they can only do so by hiring competent management, retaining their abilities, and providing them with the remuneration necessary to not only feed and educate their families but also to make them some of the most financially stable individuals within the community. If you pay them well, they won't steal from the institution. If you pay them well, they will be more loyal than Fido the dog.

PROVIDING THE MONEY

Banks and thrifts are money machines. They provide financial resources to the community so that residents, businesses, and governments can finance necessary projects. It is the responsibility of the board of directors of community banks and thrifts to provide the funds necessary to operate the financial intermediary in such a manner as to enable achievement of the goals and objectives of the institution. If the board of directors is stingy as to budgetary requests, capital expenditures, and the provision of new employees, then the bank or thrift may not be able to provide the products or services necessary to meet the needs of the community, and if it fails to do so in the long run, it will not survive as an independent institution. Thus, it is the responsibility of the board of directors to provide the resources necessary to meet the needs of the community, and in doing so, they guarantee the survivability of their financial institution, vis-à-vis others. Thus, the board of directors should independently analyze budgetary requests and utilize their experience, education, and common sense to assist in the development of budgets that permit for financial success within the community.

SELLING YOUR BANK/THRIFT

As in Chapter 8's discussion of sales and marketing, it is the function of the board of directors to promote the sales and marketing culture within your financial institution. This has to be done through written policies disseminated to the management and staff indicating that (1) sales culture is paramount to the survivability of the institution and (2) failure to provide proactive sales management will result in termination of employment. If the bank/thrift personnel wish to sit in their offices, perform their duties, and not be proactive within the community, then they must be replaced by others who will do so. It is up to the directors to make sure that the sales and marketing culture is carried out throughout the bank/thrift so that the community will benefit from a proactive, interested, and wholly involved staff of the institution that is integrally involved with the development and vitality of the community.

COMPLIANCE

The board of directors must insist on complete compliance with all state and federal statutes, rules, and regulations. There must be zero tolerance in order for your community bank/thrift to survive. You must insist that management and staff remedy all deficiencies, and failure to do so will terminate employment. The buzz word today is *total compliance*, and the board of directors is responsible for making sure your institution achieves it. There are no rewards for substantial compliance. There are only rewards of not having the regulatory agencies on your back for total compliance. Besides, if you want to do something like start a branch, buy a bank, or go interstate, you must be in total compliance. There is no ability to expand without being in conformity. This may change in the years to come, but as of now, your role as a board member is to make sure that you have remedied all deficiencies and are operating as a bank/thrift in total compliance with all consumer, community reinvestment, and fair lending statutes, rules, and regulations.

REVIEWING EXAMINATIONS AND AUDITS

An important technique is to review, analyze, and remedy all examination report deficiencies and audit deficiencies. An informed board of directors is an excellent board of directors. You should review the examination reports independently of each other, and spend at least one meeting discussing results of the examination and formulating response thereto. Management should be delegated the duty of remedying the deficiencies, preparing the reports, and keeping the board informed. The board should set up an audit/compliance committee to work with the management to make sure that all deficiencies are remedied. Whether they come from the examination report or from the certified public audit of your books and records, the board should hold the management accountable for all such remedies. If you quickly react to examination and audit report deficiencies, your financial institution will stay away from significant weaknesses that might bring on administrative orders. You can survive much better if you are a strong, safe financial institution than if you are weak, faced with administrative orders, and on the regulators' "black list." Thus, quick response to examination and audit deficiencies is a sound technique by which to survive.

RECOMMENDATIONS

- The board of directors is in charge of the financial institution.
- The management serves at will for the board of directors.
- The board of directors is the supervisor and monitor of the institution; directors are not day-to-day managers.
- Directors who are not active, participative, prepared, or in attendance should be removed through resignation and/or retirement.
- It is the responsibility of the board of directors to hire, retain, and fire management, especially the president/CEO; competent management is the key to the survival of the community banking institution.
- Employ all outside resources necessary (e.g., consultants, attorneys, accountants) to operate a safe and solvent financial institution.
- Compliance with all regulatory and auditing deficiencies is to be accomplished immediately. The directors are responsible for such remedial actions being implemented.

Management Competency and Compensation

The first line of defense for the survival of your community bank/thrift is the availability and the utilization of competent management. Without competent management, you are dead! This chapter talks about how to attract competent management, how to retain them, and how to compensate them more than adequately.

RATIONALE FOR COMPETENT MANAGEMENT

We are no longer in the banking environment that permits us to continue to employee Reliable Old Harry or Conscientious Tilly the Teller unless they are on top of their game under the most competent management and staff that you have. As community bankers, we are no longer a repository for incompetent, untrained, unmotivated nerds and drones who need to be replaced. It is quite obvious that the banking industry no longer is the source for lifetime employment regardless of merit. Since bankers of all ages and ranks serve at the pleasure of the board of directors, there is no excuse for incompetent management and staff within your financial institution. If your staff is incompetent, it is a direct reflection on the board of directors and their ability to supervise and direct the institution.

Banking is a competitive industry. It can be said that the godfather of today's commercial banking and thrift management was Charles Darwin. Indeed, survival of the fittest is the nature of the industry. Your bank or thrift has no economic right to survive. Your only chances for survival are based upon long-standing financial performance and outstanding financial condition. You cannot achieve that with a management that is not up to current standards or perhaps even slightly ahead of the curve.

Even though I mentioned in the last chapter that the board of directors is in charge of the financial institution, let's talk reality day to day. Your senior management and staff operate the bank/thrift. Without competent personnel, your institution will be weak and perhaps even fail over the long run. Even if it doesn't fail, it might be competitively out of touch with the marketplace and not compete advantageously with other financial intermediaries. Day-to-day competent management is the key to your survival, and it is the job of the board of directors to make sure that such management is recruited, retained, and compensated more than adequately in order for them to provide the foundation for survival.

Realistically, senior management works 160 to 240 hours a month on your behalf. As bank and thrift director you probably spend 10 hours per month at the most in your official capacity as directors. Unfortunately, this 10 hours includes reading at home, seminars, board meetings, and committee meetings. If this allegation of a puny 10 hours makes you mad, let it be so. If you work 20 to 30 hours per month, congratulations—you are the exception. Recently, I was facilitating a strategic planning retreat and the directors got mad when I said they only spent 10 hours per month on their institution. Three of them insisted that they spent at least 30, but they had to admit that at least half that time was on the road driving to and from their homes to the board meetings. Do I need to mention that these individuals lived a minimum of 75 miles away from the bank, and over the month had to travel more than they worked on behalf of the bank simply because they did not live within the service area? But that is an exception—most directors live within the market served by the financial institution.

Let's look at this another way—management has 16 to 24 times as much time to operate on behalf of the bank/thrift as you do as directors. Every hour that you spend in the bank/thrift, you are giving 100 percent effort on behalf of your institution. If you give the same credit to your senior management, they are spending 16 to 24 times as much time on behalf of the institution, giving 100 percent effort. The downside is obvious: If they are incompetent, they have 16 to 24 times as much chance to louse up the bank's condition and to provide inferior financial performance, leadership, supervision, asset and quality internal control, and quality consumer compliance as you do since you are only there 10 hours per month. They can get into a lot more trouble in 240 hours per month than you can in 10 hours even if you work at it diligently. Thus, if I wanted active, competent management in my financial intermediary, I would want the most competent management I could afford and then let them put in 16 to 24 times as much time as I spent and they would then become my first line of defense against irregularities, embezzlements, inferior financial performance, unsafe and unsound banking practice, and violations of law. Three cheers for competent management, which is hardworking 16 to 24 times as much as I am.

DIRECTOR'S ROLE

A close, personal friend of mine who also happens to be a competitor, Mr. Richard B. Foster of BanConsult, Lansing, Michigan, often says that the board of directors only has two jobs: Hire the president and fire the president. This may be an oversimplification, but it may pinpoint the most important function the board of directors has. We demand and insist upon competent management; then the president/CEO represents such competency. If he is not competent, he must be the first to go. You don't fire the team, you just fire the manager. One of the most important functions that you have as a board of directors is to evaluate annually the qualifications, qualities, and job performance of your president/CEO and, in turn by implication, the performance of your senior and junior officers. All such officers serve at the will of the board of directors of commercial banks and thrifts, and you hold the power of life and death for them in terms of their livelihood as a banker. If you go on year after year without evaluating your president, vis-à-vis other presidents of peer group financial institutions, you are not performing your function as a board member and, even worse, you are not providing the constructive criticism and atta-boys that assist your president/CEO in becoming a better manager and administrator of your institution.

A CPA firm and various financial institution consulting firms can provide you with management evaluation systems. You can get as technical and mechanical as you desire. First, however, you have to do an annual evaluation. The best way to determine how well your president/CEO is doing is to (1) compare him/her with leaders at comparable peer group banks and thrifts within your marketplace and (2) get an overall perception of how your employees, townspeople, customers, and investors are dealing with your president and vice versa. All of us have assets and liabilities, and no one should expect their president to be perfect. On the other hand, if you are pushing for sales culture but your president hides in his office, you have a problem! If your staff is scared of your president, hates your president, and/or avoids him/her with a passion, you have a problem. If your staff thinks your president is not fair and perhaps is acting not only unethically but possibly dishonestly, you have a big problem. You can determine the qualifications of your president/CEO by simply keeping your eyes and ears open as you operate as a director.

You should set goals and objectives for the bank/thrift to accomplish. Your president is the administrative officer responsible for their implementation. If he cannot implement such goals and objectives year after year, it is time to replace him since he is not a strong administrator. Deviations from plan are expected, but year in and year out your president/CEO should accomplish the goals and objectives set out by the board of directors and implemented by the senior management and staff. Evaluation of the president is a crucial function of the board of directors in keeping the community bank/thrift in such a position that it can survive through safe and solvent banking.

FRIENDSHIPS

Is your board stacked with friends of the president? Are you a member of the board of directors that was selected by the president? Your answer is probably yes to at least one of these two questions. Shareholders do not select directors. Bank and thrift presidents select directors. Then, it should not come as a surprise that bank presidents/CEOs last a long time since the directors are reluctant to remove them even when their performance as chief administrators is less than adequate. Being a member of the board of directors in a for-profit corporation that just happens to be a community bank or thrift is a responsible position that overshadows friendships regardless of whether you have known the president since grade school or have married into his/her family. The president should be evaluated on a regular basis regardless of friendship or other relationship. In a majority of cases, it is the president/CEO who puts the board of directors into a legal bind. It is not the other way around. You should respect your president/CEO for her abilities, but you should not be blind to her liabilities. If the bank/thrift runs into a financial condition problem, inferior financial performance, or unsafe and unsound banking practices, the state and federal regulatory agencies look to the board of directors to solve the problem. They do not look to the bank/thrift president/CEO. They expect you to have kept the president/CEO in line and to have employed a competent individual to do the job. If you are in trouble with the state and federal regulatory agencies, it is your president's problem and she either has to correct the problem or find other employment.

MANAGEMENT SUCCESSION

Bank and thrift presidents do not stay on the job forever. If they don't retire, they become ill or disabled. Finally (this possibility is never thought about by the directors), they might get a better job somewhere else and just flat leave you. Management succession becomes critical so that your financial institution can continue to operate efficiently and productively.

Look around your bank/thrift and answer the following question honestly: If something happened to the president/CEO so that he could not continue, do we have somebody on board who could step in and do the job as well? Perhaps you had better ask a less encompassing question: Do we have somebody who could step in and operate as president/CEO in an interim capacity until we find somebody from outside? If the answer is yes to the first question, you are in fantastic shape—immediately go to the next subsection of this chapter and ignore the rest of this subsection. If the answer was no to the first question but yes to the second question, then you are in fairly good shape and you should have a written plan that outlines what you can do in case your president becomes disabled or leaves. The interim person can then run the financial institution until you have hired a person from outside. It is not unfair to let someone internal know that he can be an interim executive officer but is not expected to be the long-term officer. This is especially true if the individual happens to be 60 to 65 years of age and his career will soon end in retirement.

However, if the answers to both questions in the above paragraph were no, then you are in deep trouble. This means that your financial institution has only one senior officer who can chew gum and talk at the same time. You have no management succession program. You have no plan for shifting from your current president to a new executive officer. If something happens to your president, you will be shell-shocked. You will be in catatonic arrest. The board of directors will be incapable of making solid plans immediately because they have no focus on what they should do. This is an extreme problem that may result in taking on administrative orders or regulatory sanctions based upon inferior performance and lack of quality. You as a director don't want that.

You should develop a management succession program among yourselves. You can include the president/CEO if she is old enough that you think she is going to retire or die on the job, rather than simply move on. You want her opinion as to the qualities of the other managers, but you don't necessarily want her to handpick her successor. Furthermore, you might want to do this alone if you are of the opinion that the president/CEO will be against the promotion of senior officers to executive vice president, or oppose the hiring of an outside manager to come in behind the president/CEO. Over the years, most bank/thrift presidents that I have run into have been relatively insecure—especially if they did not have an employment contract. Since employment contracts at the bank level are often not in vogue, or even legal in some jurisdictions, some community banks/thrifts have contracts for their presidents at the holding company level. This is one way to make your president more secure if you decide to bring in additional management behind her to deepen and broaden your management team.

You should develop a written plan for hiring management succession if you don't believe that you have the internal candidates already on hand. For example, let's use the illustration of a 55-year-old president, with a 68-year-old executive vice president. The executive vice president is going to retire in two years, leaving a void. Obviously the president is not planning to retire for almost 10 to 15 years. Now you look around the management and find out you have one individual 40 years of age who is not a candidate and three others(ages 31, 29, and 26) who may become candidates. You may have the world's longest management succession program, not a realistic, pragmatic management succession program, when the executive vice president retires. It may be best for you to plan to bring in a new executive vice president when the executive vice president retires or one year before retirement, and hire this new executive vice president in the age range of 55 to 60 so that he does not become a threat to the long-term careers of your younger members of management. With the right successions between the board and the junior management, and with the appropriate remuneration, this type of transition can take place.

Over my 30 years as a bank consultant, more than several times I have seen community banks/thrifts throw in the towel when their president/CEO died or retired. The board of directors had not planned for succession. There was nobody available in the institution to be a successor. Instead of looking for someone, they simply sold to vulturous bidders who circled the carrion after the president left. The worst possible thing is to have a director take over as president. Once the director becomes president, you can't beat him out of the job with a stick. Furthermore, a former director may have no clue how to be a professional banker; this often is worse than having nobody as president. Furthermore, after the new president has been selected, the old director can't get back to his previous position as a director and usually meddles around in the management of the bank/thrift. It is not very difficult to develop a management succession program and know how to implement it when a disaster takes place. You don't have to anticipate that the worst will occur—it just makes common sense as a board of directors and as senior management to make sure that in case of disaster (i.e., disability or death of the president/CEO) you have a smooth means by which to either promote from within or buy someone from outside while the institution doesn't miss a beat. To do less than that is to fail your responsibilities as directors.

MANAGEMENT RECRUITMENT

There are really only two ways to have a competent management. You either grow it yourself or buy it from outside. As board members, you are responsible for doing both. When you need to determine management succession or, even worse, pick a new president/CEO as successor to a previous president, then either you have the talent inside ready to flower or you have to go outside to buy it. Hopefully, you will have the next president waiting in the wings with his nicest outfit on ready to give the acceptance speech. However, if you don't, then you need to figure out how to recruit competent management to take over. This analysis is just as good for second and third spots as it is for the first spot on your team, so this information is applicable to hiring not only a new president but also other senior officers.

Community banks and thrifts often complain that they have a hard time attracting senior management. The usual reason why the attraction is so difficult is the nature of the communities being served by the bank/thrift. If that is true in your location, then the first step in management recruiting is to determine whether there are any bankers out in the professional marketplace who came from your area. You should determine whether there are bankers now working in Oklahoma who came from Wisconsin, or bankers now working in Maine who actually came from your local town in Ohio. If they are, then they may become excellent candidates for your new position.

Second, the olden days of gentlemen's agreements as to the nonhiring of other people in town is gone. Every banker in the marketplace is free game today. Why would you pick up an unknown quantity if you could hire away your competitor's executive vice president since you know him/her from church, school meetings, and social events? Senior managements working within your market area at other financial institutions should be considered as prime candidates for your open position. You probably know more about them, their assets, their liabilities, and their overall reputation within the marketplace than you'll ever know about someone you hire from outside whom you simply interview and then check references and pray he will be excellent.

Third, assuming that there are not choices available from either inside staff, people who originally came from your community and are working elsewhere, or competitor managements, then you have to spread your net wide across the waters. You can do this job yourself, or you can have it hired out with a specialized banking/savings and loan executive placement service. If you do it yourself, you can place an ad in *The Wall Street Journal* edition that covers your area or in *American Banker*. After you have placed the ad, then you can duck. The last time I placed an ad on behalf of one of my clients, we received over 800 responses. You could talk to your state trade associations and find out if there are any bankers wandering around there who need a job; you'll find plenty of them since there are more bankers in supply than there are in demand. Or you can hire the specialized banking employment agency to do the preliminary work for you. Both approaches cost you. The former costs you in time since you will have to weed out all of the resumes down to a group to interview, interview them, bring finalists in for the job, and so on. The latter will cost you because you will pay the employment agency a fee approximating one-third of the first year's salary for the individual hired, but all the preliminary screening will be done by the employment agency and it will handle all the preliminaries until you get into the semifinals, when you get a list of candidates to review before interviewing the finalists. This costs more money, but it takes far less time. You have to decide which is more important in your operation. Furthermore, if you are replacing the president/CEO, then the recruitment of the new president becomes the job of the board of directors. If you are a typical community bank and/or thrift board, you do not have the time to do extensive advertising, analyze all of the resumes, contact individuals who make it into the semifinals, cross-check references, and handle the finalists. It is probably far more prudent to utilize the specialized banking/thrift employment service than it is to try to do the job yourself, without any experience or expertise in the field.

I can guarantee you that once you have gone through the outside management recruitment process one time, you will be far more interested in growing your own talent from within. It is a lot easier to hire management at the junior or middle management level and then groom them to become senior management and possibly the CEO in the long run. You are able to buy them cheaper, train them the way you want to train them, and end up with a product that you like. There is no guesswork as to whether the person will succeed.

MANAGEMENT COMPENSATION

Community banks and thrifts are cheap. Probably the best way for a community bank/thrift president to get a salary increase is to quit and then get rehired as a new president. There is a tendency for boards of directors of community banks and thrifts not to pay going market rates for current senior and junior management. Once the management gets on board, they are nickeled and dimed to death, year after year, as they proceed up the ladder of success within the financial institution. Part of the problem results from the board of directors not knowing what appropriate salary levels should be; another part of the problem is environmental. Within the community, bankers are often some of the best paid individuals. Look at a typical board of directors of a community bank/thrift—many of these individuals are not wealthy and do not make significant incomes annually. I have been at board meetings when the president's salary was not going to be raised since nobody in the county ever makes a large amount of money. One time, when we were trying to hire a new president, several members of the board flatly refused to hire the individual because he was asking for too much money, although the salary agreed upon was flat dab on the average of the peer group. Boards of this ilk are mentally deficient. If you demand competent management, you have to pay for it. When you pay under market compensation to your management, you get less than competent management. Moreover, if you have an excellent CEO who is being paid insufficiently, this individual has a greater probability of leaving for another employment opportunity rather than staying at your shop. The worst way to retain competent management is to underpay them and think that you are saving just a few bucks so that the shareholders will benefit. An underpaid, unhappy management will cost your shareholders more in the long run. Appropriate management compensation is critical to your retention of quality management. Needless to say, the competent banking professional did not take the job with this Neanderthal-thinking board.

If you are concerned about salaries and fringe benefit costs, you might attempt, over time, to make your employees more productive (e.g., more millions of dollars of assets per employee), and pay them all well. Technology enables increased computerization, networking, electronic mail, automatic lending and operational systems, and ATMs. Thus, if you are not somewhere between $2 million and $3 million per employee, you are probably inefficient. Translated into English, pay each of your employees more and have fewer employees.

Peer group studies are available in every state for banks and thrifts to show average compensation per job function for financial institutions of your size. You can subscribe to these services and also national salary surveys so that you have a foundation on which to base your executive compensation. Moreover, if you have a quality financial institution (e.g., a CAMEL 1 or 2 or MACRO 1 or 2 bank/thrift), your senior management should be paid more than the average. Remembering that averages are only averages, and that there are plenty of salaries above the average and some below the average, you should determine how much above the averages your senior management should have their compensation based upon the financial condition and performance of your institution. For example, a community financial institution that is a CAMEL 1 or MACRO 1 should have executive compensation for the president/CEO, executive vice president, and senior vice presidents at least 25 percent above the peer group average. You must reward your outstanding management with outstanding compensation. If you are a CAMEL 3 institution, you should be at the averages. If you are a CAMEL 4 or 5 institution, or the equivalent MACRO 4 or 5, you probably need new management. At that point the peer group averages don't mean much.

You should also determine as best you can competitive salaries within your market area. Many of the financial institutions are your same size. It makes no sense to attempt to compare your salaries with multinational, money center financial institutions, but you should compare yourself with other banks and thrifts that are basically your size. Again, comparing your quality with their quality and comparing their salaries with your salaries will give you a strong idea of where your executive salary should be.

Except for the president's salary, the board of directors should delegate salary considerations to the president/CEO. The board of directors should act as a review body for salaries of senior officers and employees, and may act as a grievance body in case some of the bankers are unhappy with their salaries. The president/CEO's salary is the responsibility of the board of directors. It should be set annually by an ad hoc committee established by the board, which should, year after year, review the achievements, goals and objectives, and performance of the president/CEO in order to determine next year's compensation. There is no way to delegate this, and it certainly should be more than a simple cost-of-living adjustment done at one board meeting. If you have a quality senior management, you should retain them through appropriate compensation.

MANAGEMENT FRINGE BENEFITS

Your bank/thrift president should live in one of the nicest homes within your community. Your president should be one of the best paid administrators within your banking market. Your bank president is a human being who may (or may not) marry, raise a family, educate children, and prepare for retirement and estate planning. The tendency for community bank/thrift directors to pay less than market rate compensation to their president/CEO is a fatal flaw. Your president/CEO should be one of the best compensated individuals and, as such, will perform admirably for you.

I often say in my speeches that if you don't pay your president enough, he/she might steal the place. If they are paid well and have material fringe benefits, they know that every dollar of expense is cents out of their shareholdings and can adversely impact their compensation. You want your bank president to think twice when he/she is making a decision: What impact will this decision have upon the book value of our financial institution and therefore my stock options, my fringe benefits in general, and my overall compensation? You want your management tied integrally with your financial institution so that the leadership of the CEO provides the impetus for an outstanding financial condition and an excellent financial performance.

The most commonly utilized fringe benefits for presidents/CEOs are stock options, deferred compensation, life and health insurance plans, country club and other club memberships, and bank cars. These should all be considered as regular compensation, and should be based upon performance of the financial institution. Again, if you are a CAMEL 1 or 2 bank or a MACRO 1 or 2 savings and loan, your management has performed admirably, and your financial institution is financially safe and solvent and has performed above peer group levels. Why then not give stock options for such incentive performance as well as provide deferred compensation for the individuals after retirement? Many of the defined benefit and defined contribution pension plans in place at your financial institutions will not provide a quality retirement for your senior officers. Deferred compensation can provide such quality retirement and can be backed by life insurance policies on the individuals involved. Stock options are important since the ownership of the community bank or thrift provides an incentive for better performance year after year, and gives the president/CEO an exit vehicle providing for outstanding financial well-being upon retirement or when the financial institution is sold. Life and health insurance policies are also important as fringe benefits since they provide for quality retirement and estate planning. A bank car for the president/CEO is almost a necessity these days since, as we saw in earlier chapters, your president/CEO is on the road almost 50 percent of the time within the community, is emersed in state and national trade association work on your behalf, and is involved in economic and financial leadership within the market. All of these require travel, and the bank car can be determined as a necessary fringe benefit for their use.

Fringe benefits are also noted by the statewide compensation surveys done by state bank and thrift trade associations as well as by private companies that sell fringe-benefit–oriented services. As you analyze the fringe benefit package for your senior management, make sure that you know what others are being offered within your marketplace and throughout your state so that you can offer fringe benefits comparable to other financial institutions. This will keep your senior management comfortable and pleased with their current environment rather than looking elsewhere for new livelihoods.

In summary, fringe benefits are an important element of the total compensation package to your senior management. It is really no different than the coach at the university who gets a basic salary of $110,000, but is permitted to endorse certain items, sponsor basketball or football camps, and have a radio or TV show. Your president/CEO should have a basic salary, have the opportunity to earn incentive performance-oriented bonuses, and at the same time have fringe benefits based upon performance as well as position. The most expensive thing that can happen to you is to lose your president and have to hire a new one, simply because you were cheap—your chairman being called Jack Benny.

RECOMMENDATIONS

- If you don't pay them, they will go.
- Utilize peer group surveys to determine the value of your president/CEO and other senior management.
- Comparison of salaries and fringe benefits for senior managements within your banking market is necessary.
- Reward your president/CEO and other senior management for financial conditions and performance above peer group averages.
- Sell stock to your senior officers. The more they own, the more it's their place.
- Stock options and phantom options for mutuals give ownership to your management based upon performance.
- Management compensation should be greater than peer group averages in order to retain your community bank personnel.
- Recruit senior management through ties to the community, from inside, or from outside if no successors are available.
- Utilize outside specialized executive placement recruiters rather than attempting to do the job yourself. They do it better and the fee is not that high.

CHAPTER 15

Board and Management Education

An uneducated board or management is a time bomb ticking in your bank/thrift. If they don't know what's going on, how can they make rational, prudent business decisions? Board and management education is vital to the function of the individuals who supervise and monitor the financial institution as well as those who manage it on a day-to-day basis. As we shall discuss in this chapter, sources of information are different for board members than for professional management and staff, but the need for education is paramount for both groups, and the amount of education is even more critical for the professional management than for the board.

The board must be trained to understand the duty and responsibility of board members, how to delegate responsibility to the management and staff, and how to monitor the results of day-to-day performance. In essence, the board of directors must learn how to supervise and direct. There is no need for the board to learn how to manage—that is the job of the management. On the other hand, not only must management learn how to manage, but over time it must be re-educated to learn how to manage better. Administration of a financial institution involves not only the control of financial condition and performance, but also day-to-day handling of people who are the major assets of the bank/thrift. Finally, management is not only an administration, but is also made up of specialized people who have functional backgrounds in banking, accounting, and finance. Thus, not only does management continue to be educated on general administrative assignments and techniques, but it must also continue to be educated and re-educated on current FASB pronouncements, IRS rules and regulations, state and federal regulatory rules and regulations, financial theories, new Wall Street techniques, and so on. Education of the staff is an ongoing process that only quits when the individual retires from the bank/thrift.

READING YOUR WAY TO KNOWLEDGE

Directors and management have the opportunity to become more knowledgeable through reading general newspapers (such as *The Wall Street Journal*, *Barron's*, and *American Banker*) or, in contrast, weekly, monthly, and less-frequently published state and national trade association newsletters, faxes, and journals/magazines which provide information on current topics of interest, laws, new IRS rulings and regulations, and general futuristic technological advances. The board of directors and senior management should read four to five hours a week *minimum*; the remainder of the staff should be reading several hours a week, regardless of their function within the financial institution. You can only do this if you have the sources of information available. This chapter ends with a listing of relevant board of director and management education sources that are not terribly expensive for purposes of educating, re-educating, and/or continuously updating your staff and directorship at minimum cost. You do not need all of these at your bank or thrift, but a good selection of them would be a valuable asset to your board and management. It is far better to get 6, 10, or 15 different journals, newsletters, and magazines than simply get 15 copies of one journal, newspaper, or magazine. You might need three to five copies of each, but the more sources of information you have, the better off you are in getting different perspectives, viewpoints, and appraisals of what is going on in your industry.

The bibliography is broken into sections for your information. The first section is professional books published throughout the United States covering education for bank and thrift directors. This section is followed by national journals, newspapers, and finally, local and regional state association journals and magazines, newsletters, and organizations that can assist you in increasing your director's knowledge. These bibliographical sources can increase your education and make you a better manager/director who is thus better able to fully understand your responsibilities as they apply to your specific function within the bank/thrift.

NATIONAL, REGIONAL, AND LOCAL CONVENTIONS, CONFERENCES, SEMINARS, AND WORKSHOPS

National and state trade associations as well as proprietary corporations provide outstanding board and management education throughout the United States. Time and space do not permit a listing of these opportunities, but every national convention, state convention, or regional meeting is jam-packed with educational programs as well as golf outings, tours, and social events. In the past decade, there has been a tremendous emphasis by the national and state trade associations, such as the American Bankers Association (ABA), the Independent Bankers Association of America (IBAA), and America's Community Bankers as well as their state association affiliates and allies to provide meaningful, professional education day after day during their conventions. Do not forget these types of programs when you are attempting to increase the board and management education at your institution.

Proprietary corporations such as Sheshunoff Informational Services, Inc., the Southwestern Graduate School of Banking (SWGSB), Executive Enterprises, Inc., Banking Law Institute, and the New York Law Journal Seminar Press provide seminars and workshops throughout the United States as do the national and state associations as well as other proprietary corporations. These seminars are specialized, usually last one or two days, and are located in multiple sites around the country. You are inundated as board and management members with such program brochures, and these can be of great assistance to you if you need additional education on a specialized topic. As you can imagine, many of these are located in warm-weather climes during the winter and northern climes during the summer. They also are available in big-city arenas, on cruises, and overseas so that you can have a good time while you are learning. If you want to ensure that everybody learns, just make sure that they come back and present the results of their academic activities in the seminar or workshop.

SCHOOLS

Most of you are familiar with banking schools. However, a refresher does not bother us. If you are a commercial banker, there are a series of banking schools available for you throughout the United States:

1. Stonier Graduate School of Banking, sponsored by the American Bankers Association, located at the University of Delaware (Newark, Delaware) but not associated with the University of Delaware.
2. Bank of the South (Louisiana State University in Baton Rouge).
3. Graduate School of Banking (University of Wisconsin in Madison).
4. Western Graduate School of Banking (University of Colorado in Boulder).
5. Southwestern Graduate School of Banking (Southern Methodist University in Dallas).
6. Pacific Rim Banking School (University of Washington in Seattle).

These are general management leadership and educational programs. In addition, universities such as Harvard and Columbia have advanced management schools for commercial bankers. The Center for Banking Excellence, Fairfield University in Fairfield, Connecticut, has been the nucleus for education at mutual savings banks, federal savings banks, and savings and loans at the various state trade associations and the nationally oriented America's Community Bankers. In addition to these general schools, the ABA, IBAA, and ACB have specialized schools such as commercial loan schools, advanced commercial loan schools, mortgage schools, trust schools, and consumer loan schools located throughout the United States. Recently, several national trade associations as well as the American Association of Bank Directors and the National Association of Bank Directors have been attempting to certify directors of banks and thrifts through director education at one-week or two-week schools throughout the country. All of these are available to you as sources for additional education on a specialized basis; you receive a certificate of achievement upon completion. There is seldom a day that goes by that, when reviewing a resume of a professional banker, I don't see proudly outlined in the resume the fact that the individual graduated from Stonier, Wisconsin, Bank of the South, or some such. These banking schools are tough. They take dedication and a lot of work—and your people benefit by their programs. They make your management more competent, and a more competent, management makes your community bank/thrift survive in a complex, uncertain market. Furthermore, many of these schools are attuned to the community bank/thrift mentality since the larger banks and thrifts in this country have their own in-house educational programs. Thus, these schools are really closer to the environment and the ambiance of your institution than they are to the "big boys," and your people learn about what goes on across the country in other peer-group–type banking institutions.

LOCAL EDUCATION

As I have traveled around the country, I have run across a lot of local banking education. State and regional universities and colleges provide accounting, finance, and management education, and some have geared up to assist bank and thrift personnel to work toward their undergraduate degrees with specializations in banking. In addition, community and technical colleges provide post–high-school education; many teach the basics of accounting, finance, and economics to assist banking personnel. The American Institute of Banking operates in many communities within this country, utilizing professional bankers to assist as professors and lecturers to bank and thrift personnel who are currently working within the institutions. This provides a foundation for continued professional education, especially since many of the personnel do not have college educations. Even those who do have college educations may not have a background in accounting, finance, economics, or management, which can be provided to them through local colleges, universities, technical schools, and AIB programs. The prudent community bank/thrift that wishes to survive will utilize all local sources of education available to promote its staff's competence.

IN-HOUSE SEMINARS

By far the biggest bang for your buck comes from holding an in-house seminar. This seminar can be designed to assist the board of directors in upgrading their education or you can utilize the in-house seminar for strategic planning purposes or to assist your accounting staff in understanding new rules and regulations, internal control changes, and so on. In-house seminars are more efficient because more people can attend, at a mutually convenient location and time, and more pressure can be placed upon the employees and directors to be at these seminars. Furthermore, they are extremely cost-efficient because all you have to do is hire the speaker to come to you rather than sending all of your employees to see the speaker. Furthermore, you can control the content of the program and, at the same time, the presentation can be far more specific if it is held in your shop than if it is held at the state capital in a hotel ballroom. Presenters of the seminars can review your financial information and provide you with advice and comments specifically upon the current local situation at your financial institution rather than making generic comments that fit all participants in the audience. This is why you get a bigger bang for the buck: More people participate, more people are educated, and more information pertinent to your own financial institution is imparted during the seminar.

I have one caveat concerning local in-house seminars for employees. The smaller the community financial institution, the less may be the credibility of the in-house seminar. This is especially true if personnel within the organization are teaching newer employees concerning teller training, internal controls, auditing, and so on. Several years ago, my firm and I had the opportunity to assist a bank in performing a strategic plan and we ran across an entire senior management, none of whom had gone beyond high school. These individuals had never worked anywhere else and had been trained in-house on the job. They were now teaching new employees in-house on the job. Ignorance compounded is ignorance squared.

Small community banks and thrifts may not have the expertise necessary internally to provide outstanding education. Video and audio tapes purchased from national and state banking associations or from proprietary corporations may be of assistance, since these will be more educationally valuable than in-house training, but my professional experience as a consultant indicates to me that in the smallest community banks and thrifts, the best way to educate your staff is to send them out to state and national organizations, meetings, seminars, and workshops rather than attempting to spread ignorance throughout your whole bank through older, insular, and parochial employees attempting to show new staff members the ropes.

EDUCATIONAL BUDGET

Education is not free. In fact, most of the education that we have gotten free probably isn't repeatable or legal, and we certainly wouldn't want to tell it to anybody close. Banking education is not free. We must pay for it so we must budget for it. As I have operated over the past 30 years as a financial consultant, I have noticed that whenever there is a tendency to trim back expenses, the first thing to go is the educational budget at the bank/thrift. As an illustration, a major bank in Toledo, Ohio, back in the mid-1980s decided to cut its educational budget, including internships at local colleges. It eliminated 12 internships per quarter and thought that was cost-efficient. First of all, these individuals worked less than 20 hours a week and got paid $4.50 an hour, so they were not significant expenses. Furthermore, and this was not determined until after the president axed the entire program, 83 percent of all the previous interns had been hired by the bank. If you assume what it costs to go out and recruit and bring into the bank young men and women for future advancement to become officers, then an internship program that results in hiring 83 percent of the internees is a cheap college recruitment program. The educational budget should not be given the ax first—why not ax one or two people who are unproductive or could take early retirement, and utilize the funds saved from those positions to continue to educate current personnel who can become even better bankers in the long run?

For years I have lectured that a board of directors' educational budget should be at least $3,000 per director. This expense per director would cover not only conventions and conferences, but also in-house seminars and educational materials such as newsletters and trade journals. The same kind of budget should be developed for your staff. Obviously, your senior staff would be going to more comprehensive banking schools, which are far more expensive. A one-year program at a national banking school will involve at least $4,000 cash out of pocket plus obviously the time lost from the financial institution. A review of the financial ratio comparisons for banks and thrifts does not indicate any comparison of bank to peer group educational budget statistics. You cannot look on the UBPR and find an educational budget ratio. In fact, over all my years in consulting, I have never really run across any percentage on this issue. Most financial institutions I work with have a budget that is arrived at over time by simply allowing everybody to get whatever education they want, then determining what that level was last year and adding to it for this year. That is really not a bad way to handle it—as long as you maintain that educational budget when times are hard. An educational budget permits your staff to become more efficient, productive, and experienced, and that educational opportunity provides for increased enthusiasm, motivation, and loyalty to the financial institution. It is a win–win situation. If you want a ballpark number, budget for next year

$1,000 per full-time employee for education. The second year, budget $2,000 per employee. The $2,000 should be more than adequate for all staff members; if it is not, then it can be adjusted from there. Thus, a bank with 50 employees should be looking at an educational budget of at least $100,000. Assuming that the bank has $100 million in deposits, this would result in a 0.1 percent reduction in the ROA, which in the short term is significant, but in the long term may permit the bank to increase its ROA by a multiple of such costs.

HOW MUCH EDUCATION?

There are no hard rules on how much education is necessary to keep your staff competent, up-to-date, and progressive. However, I have been around long enough that I have developed my own biases and subjective opinions concerning education and the typical bank/thrift staff. I believe that if the senior management is not in a legitimate banking school (and I do not mean in a bar at the state banking convention) at least once every three years, your senior management will fall behind and become less competent in handling their senior administrative duties in your bank/thrift. Once we start talking about your executive vice president(s) and your president, we are talking about not only the national banking schools, but also Harvard's and Columbia's advanced management schools in order to make them far better administrators than they are currently. As for the staff, some training should be achieved by the staff every year. If you look at competitive industries, personnel are getting trained one to two weeks a year. The Japanese have a tendency to train their employees four weeks a year. Obviously, you cannot start out training everybody three or four weeks a year, or you won't have anybody back in the shop handling the customers and answering the phone. I believe that you should have every one of your employees involved in some meaningful educational activity at least one week a year, and that can be very flexible—such as a one-week banking school like the Ohio School of Banking, the Robert Perry School of Banking in Michigan, or a similar school in your state designed for bank employees with more than five years of experience who are not yet middle management. As your staff gets closer to middle management and are acting as supervisors and administrators of departments and functions within your bank/thrift, then you should move up their education to two weeks a year: one week that is administrative-leadership–oriented (such as supervisory training, stress training, and training on sexual harassment and how to avoid problems within the financial institution) and the other week concerning functional aspects of their bank/thrift area that they are responsible for so it will improve their personal and professional qualities. Again, some of these programs may be one-day, two-day, or three-day programs, so I am really talking about two weeks out of the office in some form of educational activity in addition to whatever you do internally, but this type of training is mandatory in order to keep your staff on pace with changes in the industry. The more educated your staff, the more proficient they are, and the fewer problems you are going to have with regulatory deficiencies, competitive pressures, and the ability to survive.

RECOMMENDATIONS

- Trained and educated directors are competent.
- Trained and educated management and staff are competent.
- Competent personnel do not kill banks/thrifts.
- Emphasis by the board of directors on education should include not only the board but all management and staff.
- Establish training programs for all staff at national, state, and local conferences, conventions, workshops, and seminars.
- Assign educational training to senior management, middle management, and staff each year.
- Every senior manager should go to a banking school every three years.
- All staff members should have one or two weeks of education per year.
- Establish an educational budget for directors (approximately $3,000 per year).
- Establish an educational budget for all staff (approximately $2,000 per full-time equivalent per year).
- Cut people rather than the educational budget if you run into hard times.

BIBLIOGRAPHY

Books

America's Community Bankers. Published in quarterly loose-leaf supplements. *Trustees & Directors Handbook*. 900 19th Street, NW, Suite 400, Washington, DC 20006.

American Law Institute. *Principles of Corporate Governance: Analysis and Recommendations*, Volumes 1 and 2, May 13, 1992.

Austin, Douglas V. et al. *Financial Institution Director Liabilities and Responsibilities*, 4th edition, Austin Financial Services, Inc., 3450 W. Central Avenue, Suite 120–124, Toledo, Ohio 43606-1403.

Austin, Douglas V. et al. *Inside the Board Room: How to Be an Effective Bank Director*, Business One-Irwin, Homewood, Illinois, 1989.

Bexley, James. *The Bank Director: A Complete and Practical Handbook*, Bankers Publishing Company, 1985.

Comptroller of the Currency. *The Director's Book: The Role of the National Bank Director*, Washington DC, August 1987.

Drinker, Biddle & Reath. *Responsibilities and Liabilities of Bank and Thrift Directors and Officers*, 1994. The Fidelity and Deposit Companies, PO Box 1227, Baltimore, Maryland 21203.

Gup, Benton E. *The Bank Director's Handbook*, 1995. Irwin Professional Publishing, 1333 Burr Ridge Parkway, Burr Ridge, Illinois 60521.

Regulatory Compliance Associates, Inc. *Guide to Preparing Board Reports*, 1990. Irwin Professional Publishing, 1333 Burr Ridge Parkway, Burr Ridge, Illinois 60521.

Statts, William F., and Shane A. Johnson. *Effectiveness of Bank Board of Directors: Evidence and Prescriptions*. Center for Professional Education, San Antonio, Texas, 1988.

Stevenson, Herbert T. *The Board of Directors: A Guide for Enhancing Your Effectiveness*, Bank Administration Institute, 1 North Franklin Street, Chicago, Illinois 60606.

Stevenson, Herbert T. *The Executive Management Guide to an Effective Board of Directors*, Irwin Professional Publishing, 1333 Burr Ridge Parkway, Burr Ridge, Illinois 60521.

National Magazines

ABA Banking Journal. Monthly magazine of American Bankers Association, 345 Hudson Street, New York, New York 10014.

America's Community Banker. America's Community Bankers, 900 19th Street, NW, Suite 400, Washington, DC 20006.

American Banker. Daily newspaper published by Thompson Publishing Corporation, One State Street Plaza, New York, New York 10004.

The Bank Board Letter. Monthly newsletter published by Bank News, 912 Baltimore Avenue, Kansas City, Missouri 64105.

Bank Director. Quarterly magazine published by National Association of Bank Directors, PO Box 3468, Brentwood, Tennessee 37024.

Bank Directors Briefing. Monthly newsletter published by ABA, 345 Hudson Street, New York, New York 10014.

Bank Directors Report. Monthly newsletter published by Warren Gorham & Lamont, 1

Penn Plaza, 40th floor, New York, New York 10119.

Bank Management. Bimonthly magazine from the Bank Administration Institute published by Faulkner & Gray, 1 North Franklin Street, Chicago, Illinois 60606.

Bank Marketing. Monthly magazine of Bank Marketing Association, 309 West Washington Street, Chicago, Illinois 60606.

Bank Systems + Technology. Monthly magazine. 1515 Broadway, New York, New York 10036.

The Bankers Magazine. Warren Gorham & Lamont, 1 Penn Plaza, 40th floor, New York, New York 10119.

Bankers Monthly. Monthly magazine, 5615 Cermak Road, Cicero, Illinois 60650.

Banking Law Journal. Warren Gorham & Lamont, 1 Penn Plaza, 40th floor, New York, New York 10119.

Directors & Trustees Digest. America's Community Bankers, 900 19th Street, NW, Suite 400, Washington, DC 20006.

Directors Digest. Monthly newsletter published by United States League of Savings Institutions, 111 East Wacker Drive, Chicago, Illinois 60601.

Economic Outlook. America's Community Bankers. 900 19th Street, NW, Suite 400, Washington, DC 20006.

Independent Banker. Independent Bankers Association of America, 1168 South Main Street, PO Box 267, Sauk Centre, Minnesota 56378-0267.

Issues in Bank Regulations. Bank Administration Institution, published by Faulkner & Gray, 1 North Franklin Street, Chicago, Illinois 60606.

Journal of Commercial Lending. Published monthly by Robert Morris Associates, One Liberty Place, Suite 2300, 1650 Market Street, Philadelphia, Pennsylvania 19103.

United States Banker. Monthly magazine published by Faulkner & Gray, Inc., 11 Penn Plaza, New York, New York 10001.

Regional Magazines

Bank News. 912 Baltimore Avenue, Kansas City, Missouri 64105.

Northwestern Financial Review. NFR Communications, Inc., 3407 West 44th Street, Minneapolis, Minnesota 55410.

Southern Banker. Thompson Publishing Corporation, One State Street Plaza, New York, New York 10004.

Newsletters

ABA state associations (all states). Monthly, bimonthly publications.

Bank Directors Report. Published by Warren Gorham & Lamont for the benefit of members of the American Association of Bank Directors, 1 Penn Plaza, 40th floor, New York, New York 10119.

IBAA state associations (all states). Monthly, bimonthly publications.

We have now come to the final chapter together. I hope you have not found it a long journey through the previous chapters on how to survive as a community bank or thrift. I have enjoyed writing this manuscript and

CHAPTER 16

The Future of Community Banks and Thrifts in the International, National, and Interstate Banking and Branching Environment

discussing the various techniques on how quality community banking organizations can provide financial leadership and survive in a competitive environment. You may ask what else is there to say, and the answer is not much. But, before we leave this book, let's look into the future on a general basis and try to tie together what you as community banks and thrifts have to consider vis-à-vis survival in an increasingly competitive, risky, international, national, and interstate banking and branching environment.

VISION

If this book has convinced you of anything, I hope it has convinced you that you must sit back and think big and long. In spite of being directors for only a few years or senior management until you retire in 1998, you must assume that your community bank or thrift is going to survive until 2010 or 2020 and beyond, and that the decisions you make today will affect the long-term financial condition and performance of your institution. You cannot simply come to monthly meetings and think only of 1996 or 1998 terms. You cannot forget the future. Someone on the team must be the long-term thinker. A few of you can specialize in sprints, one or two can throw the hammer or do the pole vault, but you must have at least one quality athlete who is your marathon runner, because that is the only way you can survive to 2020 and beyond. Vision should be much longer than your tenure on the board, and you should be thinking in terms of decades and generations—not simply months and years.

If your president/CEO is not your marathon thinker, you are in trouble. If your current president is an excellent operational banker or makes good-quality loans, but does not really plan long-term and think big, you had better work on developing a long-term marathon thinker. Perhaps it has to be the executive vice president who will take over, or you may have to bring in someone from outside into the bank/thrift to become the long-term planner and administrator of your institution. Banking is more than simply complying with current rules and regulations. Banking is much more than simply opening each morning and closing each evening. Your banking institution must be more than just a piggy bank with a hole in the front rather than in the top. Your banking institution must be a forward-thinking, long-term–planning institution that understands the crosscurrents of risk and uncertainty, competitive pressures, management fallibilities, and compliance rules and regulations in order to survive.

As a part of the direction and supervision of the community bank/thrift, visioning and strategic planning should account for approximately 10 to 25 percent of the time spent. Conditions change so quickly within the industry while pressures placed upon the industry from outside are so constant that continuous planning is vital to the future operations of your institution. It is necessary to make sure that your financial institution runs appropriately day to day and that you comply with the examiners, regulators, and all compliance deficiencies. You must meet the needs of your customers, and you must have the appropriate physical facilities to operate. In spite of all these mundane problems that affect you day to day, you must plan for the future or you will not get there.

COMPETENCY OF MANAGEMENT

We have stressed over the previous chapters the importance of competent management and staff. I am not downplaying the need for competent directors—that is a given. However, competent management and staff are there day to day, hour after hour, and are on the front line of banking every business day of the year. If they are not up to speed as to what is going on in the industry, if they do not have the talents necessary to keep competent within the industry's parameters, or if they are not motivated to perform in excellent fashion, your financial institution will suffer.

Thus, the hiring and retention of quality senior management and their hiring and retention of junior management and staff are critical to your survival. In order to determine the competency of management, you should analyze and evaluate their merits on an annual basis and provide the training and education necessary to keep them current within the industry so that they do not make operational and managerial mistakes in the ordinary course of business.

WHERE THE INDUSTRY IS GOING

Table 16–1 shows my prediction of where the financial institutions are going to be in the year 2000. I have projected the further decline and amalgamation of the industry to the year 2000, and you as readers should be aware of the continued consolidation of banks and thrifts during the remainder of this decade. Are you going to be one of the survivors? This whole book has talked about how to survive, but these numbers indicate that there will be a continued consolidation of the financial institutions industry and you are going to have to work awfully hard in order to be one of the survivors. Currently, there are about 8,500 commercial bank entities in this country, and 5,000 by the year 2000 is within strong possibility. Savings and loans at the end of 1995 numbered about 1,500, although about 200 of those were already owned by commercial bank holding companies. Ending up with only 250 independent, autonomous savings and loans by the year 2000 is also a realistic projection. Credit unions have consolidated significantly from over 21,000 in 1980 to the 12,000 level in 1996; having only 10,000 or fewer by the year 2000 is almost a certainty. Your community bank or thrift can survive only if you model the techniques outlined in the previous 15 chapters, but couple that also with the understanding that you are going to have to fight your way to the year 2000 through solid financial performance with a resultant quality financial condition. You are not going to get there simply operating day to day, 9 AM to 3 PM, and not paying any attention to the conditions around you.

Not only is the industry consolidating, but it is also changing significantly in terms of competition within and among the various types of depository financial institutions. The days of the fast-growing savings and loan industry are over. Savings and loans are, for all intents and purposes, disappearing. Thrifts are becoming banks. Community thrifts are becoming community banks. In fact, in many communities you

TABLE 16-1

Financial Institutions, 1980, 1995, 2000

Type of Institution	1980	1995	2000
Commercial banks	14,435	9,941	5,000
Savings banks	464	551	Virtually eliminated
Savings and loans	4,613	1,478	250 or fewer
Credit unions	21,467	11,887	10,000 or fewer

Source: Federal Deposit Insurance Corporation Office of Thrift Supervision

cannot tell the difference between a community bank and a community thrift anymore—their portfolios are much the same and they operate as aggressively against each other as they used to operate within their own subsections of the financial institutions industry. However, the most important change is in the consolidation of the largest commercial banking institutions and savings and loans into multistate, national organizations through interstate banking and the soon-to-be implemented interstate branching. Over the past several years, the number of mergers and acquisitions per year has increased almost twofold. Although most of these mergers and acquisitions were "big bank" mergers, (e.g., Chemical/Chase Manhattan, Wells Fargo/First Interstate, First Chicago/NBD, Fleet/Shawmut, First Union/First Fidelity), there have been a significant number of community bank and thrift mergers and acquisitions. For example, in 1994, according to *U.S. Banker*, there were 282 community bank mergers and acquisitions out of the total 334 mergers and acquisitions. This is indicative of the constant change within the banking industry. In addition, thrifts have consolidated through mergers with each other, but primarily through the sale of stock thrifts to commercial bank holding companies with continued operation as wholly owned affiliates of such holding company. As of year-end 1995, there were 200 savings and loan charters as subsidiaries of registered bank holding companies. Since thrifts and banks are not significantly different as to how they can compete in local markets, this trend is considered to be an appropriate continuing trend that will affect you as a thrift.

International banking corporations currently control over 23 percent of domestic IPC deposits within the United States, and from 250 separate banking institutions, they accommodate almost 30 percent of all commercial and industrial loans in the United States each year. International banking operations have almost 1,000 locations in the

United States and continue to be strong competitors with American domestic banks and thrifts. National banking is now permitted through interstate reciprocity, interstate banking in 49 of the 50 states. Only Hawaii does not have interstate banking of any kind. Interstate branching, permitted by the Reagle-Neal Bill in 1994 and fully implemented by June 1, 1997, is already adopted in more than 40 states in some fashion. The future of interstate banking and branching is crystal clear. The larger banking financial institutions will operate over state lines, both in affiliate and branching capacities, and will by the end of the decade be in most of the populous states within the United States. I doubt if any commercial banking organization will be in all 50 states with depository offices by the year 2000, but they don't have to be to be in 90 percent of the population centers and 95 percent of the financial centers. There are some very beautiful geographical areas of our country, which we call states, that are not at the same time financial centers. Thus, you may not find every multistate, nationally oriented commercial bank and thrift operating in Kansas, Nebraska, Montana, North Dakota, or Wyoming. You can pretty well bet your bippy that these organizations will be operating in New York, California, Illinois, Michigan, Ohio, Texas, Florida, Georgia, and other population centers throughout the country where all the financial markets are located. Already there are significant numbers of nonbanking offices operating within 50 states. For example, Chemical Bancorporation, through its own offices and those purchased through Manufacturers Hanover in 1993 as well as Chase Manhattan in 1996, operates in all 50 states with loan production offices or consumer finance offices. Citicorp operates banks and thrifts in over 20 states, and Bank One operates in more than 20 states with either depository offices or nonbanking loan production/consumer finance offices. All of these institutions will go nationwide by the year 2000 or at least enough nationwide to be in 90 percent of all the markets. Your community bank or thrift will be competing against these institutions in physical space but not in real life. They are going to be operating at a different level with different horizons than your institution, but you must still be concerned about their presence within your market.

By the time we get to the year 2000, there will be 50 nationally oriented commercial bank/thrift banking organizations operating throughout the United States. All the rest are going to be community banking and thrift organizations. Thus, out of 5,000 organizations, about 50 will be the multinational organizations operating in a different banking industry than the community banks. These 50 will be operating against financial service corporations, international banking organizations, and government lending agencies on an international and national scale, while community banks and thrifts will be operating within local banking markets as they do today. This does not mean the death of the community bank or thrift—it simply means that there will be two different banking industries and they shall be parallel to each other, not cut-throat competitors. As outlined extensively above, the multinational or national banking organization cannot kill off community banks or thrifts—it can simply make them operate more profitably and efficiently, but the larger organization will still be within the banking markets providing services to a different customer and clientele than the community bank.

TECHNOLOGY

In the next 10 to 15 years you will not be able to operate with a group of monks utilizing quill pens back in your operational areas. Technology is not only here, it is beginning to dominate the banking industry. We have gone from a labor-intensive industry to a capital-intensive industry. You will have fewer employees and more computers per million dollars of assets. Technology will drive the development of new products and services and their delivery over the next 10 to 15 years. It does not make any difference whether you are located in the midst of a city or 150 miles away from any major population center; you will have to provide a technology-driven banking service to your public in order to meet their needs. As directors and senior managers, you should not be frightened by technology. I am no longer a spring chicken, and I am not scared by technology—I just don't use it. Ignoring the fact that I am blind, I have not become computer literate over the past 20 years. However, I think I understand the value of computerization in my financial institution consulting business as well as my expert witness litigative service work and my college teaching. The only difference is that I let somebody do it on my behalf. Guess what? That is exactly what you as directors and senior managers should do with technology in your community banks and thrifts. I run across an awful lot of aging directors and managers. (I define aging as anyone who is computer illiterate, like me.) Think about this: How many younger people have you run across lately who do not have computer literacy if they have graduated from the eighth grade? So do not oppose technology and the advancement of working computers, ATM delivery systems, point-of-sale and electronic funds transfers, or Internetting your bank or thrift simply because you don't know how to do it. Technology is cheaper in the long run than human beings. On the other hand, people must interpret what the technology has provided for us, and thus technology becomes a hand maiden to your quality personnel.

PRODUCTS AND SERVICES

Chapter 12 analyzed products and services including the types of products and services you might provide in the years to come in order to be competitive. These contemplated products and services are those that are currently envisioned for community banks and thrifts, or are currently available to the industry for provision to customers, but there are going to be new products and services not even thought of today that should be available for you to provide to your customers in the years to come. The successful community bank/thrift will be analyzing new products and services as they come down the pike, year after year, in order to see whether the market needs such products and services. Market research of your banking market through demographic analysis, surveys, and focus groups will be necessary for you to determine (1) what new products and services will provide a strong, profitable bottom line to your financial institution and (2) what products and services could be eliminated in order to increase the viability of your institution. In essence, you must "think new" and be interested in providing any new product or service that will meet the needs of your customers while at the same time providing a profit to your financial intermediary. You should philosophically consider all new products and services as possible products and simply not turn away from them because you have not historically provided such services. If you do not have the people on staff that can provide such new contemplative products and services, either train your current staff or add new staff that has the expertise. Furthermore, you should eliminate those products and services that are no longer profitable and are not demanded by your customers. Perhaps elimination of such products will free up current employees to be retrained to provide the new products. If not, these employees should be replaced by new employees who can provide new products and services. Too often, new products and services are not provided to the customer simply because there is a reluctance to provide them because current staff does not understand the products and services and cannot provide them in a quality fashion. This type of reluctance to change must be eliminated in order for new products and services to be provided in a quality manner. Again, if the personnel are reluctant to change, change the personnel.

CHANGE, CHANGE, CHANGE

Change is the name of the game. Tradition is out. As you forecast the future, the most constant element will be change. Current products and services will go by the wayside. Current delivery systems will be replaced by more efficient delivery systems. Current hours of service will be expanded to become seven days a week, 24 hours a day. Banking services will be provided in supermarkets, shopping malls, ATMs, over the phone, and through the computer. There will be fewer and fewer customers coming to your main office and approaching the teller line. Your staff will need to work more flexible hours and you will have fewer full-time and more part-time customer service representatives and tellers to provide basic banking services. In essence, if you continue to operate the same way you are operating now, you will not survive. You must go back to ground zero and look at every part of your bank/thrift and decide what is being operated and delivered efficiently today, what should be improved, and, if it can be improved, how to improve it. You may need to throw away tradition and current methodology. If your current delivery system is the appropriate system, maintain it. But it must pass the benefit–cost test and it must be the best delivery system currently available. Even if you maintain it, you should review your decision in several years to determine whether it has become anachronistic. If your personnel drag their feet concerning changes in the delivery system and how they operate, then either massive retraining or massive replacement becomes essential. There are plenty of bankers in the marketplace today who have been downsized and merged out of a job. If your people resist change, they can always go sell real estate or work in a filling station. You can replace them with competent individuals. Your survival as a community bank or thrift depends upon the quality of your service delivery and such delivery is based upon the quality of your products and services, which can only be delivered through quality service of your people. Reluctant, unmotivated, and negative personnel will destroy your chances to survive in the future.

BUY OUT YOUR SHAREHOLDERS, DON'T MERGE

The greatest risk to your survival is not incompetent boards of directors, terrible management, or even state and federal regulations. It is the inability to meet the needs of your shareholders for liquidity and marketability of their common stock. Operating as a bank or thrift holding company, you have the ability to buy back the stock. If you wish to remain independent until the year 2010 or the year 2020, you must be able to shift your shareholder base from the current shareholders to newer shareholders—some of whom may not even be born yet. In order to survive, you need to plan today and have the capital available, or at least the borrowing power available, to buy out current shareholders who wish to make their common stock investment liquid.

Your shareholders may have been with you for 50 to 75 years. Your original shareholders may already have passed away and bequeathed their shares to younger family members or charities, and there may be a demand for liquidity by the descendants and beneficiaries. You can make your life a lot easier if you have set up means by which to buy out these shareholders, retire the stock, and then reissue additional stock, if necessary, to new shareholders within your banking market. Many of your current shareholders may now live well beyond the area served by your bank or thrift. This is because they are the children and grandchildren of the original shareholders and they no longer have any ties to your community. They are holding the securities because you now have given them an outstanding rate of return even from a cash dividend standpoint, but they have no loyalty to your financial institution and never will be an integral part of your customer base or board of directors, and thus should be replaced by people within the community who will assist in maintaining your viability over the next 20 years. You should plan for such transition and be ahead of the curve. You should provide your shareholders with an opportunity to get out and receive a fair price. Then you can sell the securities to new investors and maintain the strong viability of your bank/thrift. This is an essential key in the future to your survival.

SALESPERSONS

I can't leave this book without coming back to the importance of sales in a community bank/thrift. We can no longer sit in our buildings and wait for customers to wander in or to at least drive by. Our competitors are out there on the landscape every day, often every night, calling on our customers. Not only do they talk to them personally, but they talk to them by phone, fax, or computer, and we simply sit in our offices and wait for them to arrive. Our customers will no longer arrive unless we convince them that we are still the best financial source available. We must provide our customers with personal service and personal business solicitation. We must visit them in their offices, their manufacturing plants, and their retail stores. Our largest residential consumer customers should be visited, or at least called upon by phone on a regular basis. We must request their attendance at annual meetings of our bank/thrift and also invite them to luncheons, dinners, and special focus groups in order to determine their needs and to satisfy their wants.

We have to analyze our current staffs and determine which ones can sell and which ones can only take orders. We have to hire people from now on who are sales-oriented. We have to consider implementing incentive compensation programs like our competitive industry compatriots. We have to correlate compensation with productivity. We have to break traditional banking's three-piece suit, wing-tip shoes, and *Wall Street Journal* mentality. A change in culture has to start at the top. The board of directors must insist on salespersons. The senior management must implement the dictates of the board. Those on the bank's staff who are not salespersons who are in salesperson functions should be either trained or replaced. If you have room for them, bury them in the back room and do not expect senior management from them. On the other hand, if they aspire to better positions, higher pay, and career opportunities as senior management, then they must learn how to sell banking services to the public day in and day out, 24 hours a day through personal and computerized/automated/ATM services.

This may sound contradictory, but if you want to stay in business, sell. Obviously, I mean that you should sell your products and services to your customers and potential customers within the banking market, not sell out to another financial institution. In the future, there will be a stigma against your financial institution if you do not sell. Salespersons will be the leaders of your bank/thrift, not order takers.

REGULATORY COOPERATION

State and federal banking regulators are in your future. You should not expect significant deregulation in the next 10 to 15 years. As long as there is federal insurance on deposits, there will be federal regulators such as the FDIC. If you wish to survive as a community bank or thrift, don't fight city hall and don't take on the state and federal banking regulators. You should do just the opposite—embrace their examination reports and correct the deficiencies noted as quickly as possible. The more you do to comply, and the sooner you comply, the more your relationships with the state and federal banking examiners and their supervisors will be enhanced, and the impact of the regulators on your financial condition and performance will be minimized. If you are a safe and solvent community bank or thrift, and you comply with all state and federal laws, rules, and regulations, you will have very little interference from the regulatory agencies, and they will assist you in meeting the goals and objectives that you have set for yourself. Moreover, the fewer problems you have with safety and solvency as well as compliance, the more time you can spend on achieving your goals and objectives as a financial intermediary. You can spend your time doing affirmative things rather than patching up negative aspects of your financial institution. It's a win–win situation for you, and tangles with state and federal regulatory agencies are a no–win situation.

FINAL THOUGHTS

If by now you are not convinced that your community bank/thrift can survive, then you have not practiced the famous Reverend Norman Vincent Peale's "Power of Positive Thinking." Community banks can and will survive. Community banks and thrifts will be an important financial foundation for local communities throughout the country for many years to come. The face of the banking industry will change significantly, but one unrelenting certainty (the cement that holds the banking industry together) will be the local community bank and thrift serving a relatively parochial and insular market. Without such financial leadership at the local level, our economy would suffer significantly. The major banking institutions can care less about the small community and the rural area as they attempt to compete nationally and internationally. It is up to the community bank and thrift to provide that financial leadership that underpins the foundation of the intermediation process in the United States.

qualifications for, 105–106
recommendations for, 109
resistance to selling insurance, 95–96
responsibility of, 101
reviewing examinations and audits, 108
setting salaries and commissions for
    sales, 93–94
strategic planning by, 104
understanding shareholders, 32–33
visioning for the future, 134–135
Books on banking, 132
Book value, 40–41
Borrowing flexibility, 28–29
BottomLine Banking (McCoy, Frieder, and
    Hedges), 13
Branches
    and internal growth, 55–56
    and interstate branching, 136–139
    purchasing other institution's, 56–57, 58
Buckman, John, 6
Budgets
    approval by board of directors, 107
    for education, 128–130

CAMEL system, 67–68
Capital adequacy
    importance of growth and, 53
    planning for repurchase of securities,
        34–36, 42
    profitability and, 68–69, 71
    safety and solvency regulations and,
        73–74
Capital standards, 68
Center of Banking Excellence, 126
CEO; *see* President/CEO
Challenges, 3–4
Change; *see* Cultural change
Chase Manhattan, 138
Chemical Bancorporation, 138
Citicorp, 138
Commercial banking institutions,
    136–139
Commissions, 93–94
Community banks; *see also* Bank and thrift
    holding companies; Branches

advantages of, 9
assets and, 9
and bank/thrift holding companies,
    23–29
challenges for, 3–4
community involvement and, 46–48,
    50–51
continuity in leadership of, 43–44
cost effectiveness of technology, 81–87
creating visioning for, 12–14, 134–135
customer orientation of, 9–10
defined, 8–10
forced sales of, 30–31
future of, 134–144
implementing cultural change in, 61
industry trends and, 136–139
leadership advantages for, 43–44
recommendations for, 10–11
role in economic development, 48–50
traditional characteristics of, 3
valuation of securities and, 36, 37, 39–40
Community involvement, 46–48
Community leadership; *see* Leadership
Community Reinvestment Act, 75, 79
Compensation
    for board of directors, 102–103, 104
    commissions for sales, 93–94
    deferred, 121
    determining competitive management
        salaries, 118–120, 122
    for employees, 119
    fringe benefits for management, 120–122
    motivating management with, 106–107
Competition
    comparing technological needs with,
        82–84, 86-87
    and future of community banks, 134–144
    hiring the, 117
    measuring growth rate against, 52–54
    sales/marketing culture and, 60
    selecting products and services and,
        90–92
Complacency, 1–3
Compliance; *see* Regulatory compliance
Compound annual growth rate (CAGR)
    basis, 53–54

88–89
recommendations for breaking, 7
strategic planning retreats and, 20–21
transaction culture and, 59–60
within community financial institutions, 3
Training and education, 123–133
Transaction culture, 59–60
Trust departments, 89–90, 99

Uniform Bank Performance Report, 16

Valuing securities, 36, 37, 39–40
Video tapes, 128
Visioning, 12–22
    corporate mission and, 14–15

creating strategic plans, 21
developing survival strategies, 12–14
for the future, 134–135
implementing goals and objectives,
    17–18
recommendations for, 22
replanning, 18–19
and responsibility for strategic plans, 21
setting goals and objectives, 15–17
strategic planning retreats and, 19–21

Western Graduate School of Banking, 126
Workshops, 125